Hanna Boys Center

Haven of Hope

William A. Byrne

Edited by Catherine Thorpe

Dedication

Each youngster who comes to Hanna Boys Center for help is a gift from God. It is our responsibility to provide the care and guidance that will help the boy and his family heal. That we have been blessed with success for the past 50 years, and look forward to turning youth's hurt into hope in the years ahead, is attributable to our only source of funding—our generous donors—to whom this Golden Anniversary Book is dedicated.

–Father John S. Crews, Ed.D., Executive Director

Hanna Boys Center
Haven of Hope

Published by Hanna Boys Center
P. O. Box 100, Sonoma, CA 95476 U.S.A.
www.hannacenter.org

First edition printed 2000
10 9 8 7 6 5 4 3 2 1

Manufactured in the United States of America

Publisher's Cataloging-in-Publication Data
Byrne, William A., 1945 –

Hanna Boys Center: Haven of Hope / by William A. Byrne – 1st ed.
144 p. illus. cm.
Includes references and index.

ISBN 0-9676437-0-8
    Sonoma (Calif.) – history
    Santa Rosa Diocese – history
    San Francisco Archdiocese – history
    Catholic Church – California – history
    Valley of the Moon (Calif.) – history
    California – History, local

    I. Title

Printed on acid-free paper

Book design and layout by Nan Perrott.
Printing by McNaughton & Gunn, Inc.
Photographs from Hanna Boys Center archives unless credited otherwise.
Endsheets photo by Judy Reed.
Hanna Boys Center gratefully acknowledges the generosity of its board of directors and other friends
who underwrote a large portion of the production costs of this book.

Contents

Preface

The 50th anniversary of the opening of Hanna Boys Center in Sonoma's Valley of the Moon on December 5, 1949, would not have been complete without the publication of this story—a vivid and heart-warming history of this unique haven of hope from its beginning.

The book, dedicated to Hanna Boys Center's only source of funding—its donors—reveals how the deep concern, and deep faith, of a few determined prelates of the Catholic Church motivated caring citizens throughout Northern California, who raised over $1 million to build what has often been called the "Boys Town of the West."

Unlike its larger and more famous predecessor in Omaha, Nebraska, Hanna Boys Center has not had the good fortune to have an internationally distributed motion picture made about it—a film bearing its name and starring the likes of Spencer Tracy and Mickey Rooney.

Which makes the unqualified success of the comparatively unknown Hanna Boys Center during its first half-century all the more remarkable.

In addition to its loyal donors, Hanna's stars have included a gifted trio of qualified priests as executive directors, and the clerics serving as their assistants; the Sisters of St. Francis; the knowledgeable professional men and women volunteers serving on the board of directors; and staff members and workers in every capacity. Plus the biggest stars of all—the boys!

All of the aforementioned personages, and their roles at Hanna, are what this book is all about.

Finally, it should be noted that despite the wealth of information, many names and photographs contained herein, some omissions were necessary due to space limitations.

It is the hope of the author and those who assisted him that the materials finally selected meet with the approval of all who read Hanna Boys Center, Haven of Hope—and that we will be forgiven for our omissions.

Robert M. Lynch
Publisher, The Sonoma Index-Tribune and Member of
    the Hanna Boys Center Board of Directors

Introduction

"I recall, either you or Father O'Connor made the statement, that you want the school to be the best of its kind in the country. We join you in this determination."

These words, written by Mother Mary Bartholomew to Monsignor William J. Flanagan on November 3, 1947, immediately set the standard of excellence which has become the hallmark of Hanna Boys Center for more than 50 years.

In his first letter to Mother Bartholomew, in which he invited the members of the Order of the Sisters of St. Francis to staff its school, Monsignor Flanagan explained the purpose of the Center:

"Archbishop Mitty has established a small home for boys in Menlo Park, which is called Hanna Center for Boys. The purpose of establishing this home was to care for boys who are underprivileged and who do not seem to fit into foster homes or large institutions. It is not intended for the real delinquent boy. However, some of our youngsters are quite upset and confused because of the early treatment that they have received."

ORIE DAMEWOOD

"Each youngster who comes to Hanna Boys Center for help is a gift from God."

—Father John S. Crews

In 1944, Monsignor William J. Flanagan, director of Catholic Charities in the San Francisco Archdiocese, and Father William L. O'Connor, assistant director, were charged by Archbishop John J. Mitty to find a home for "orphaned" and rejected boys. This directive was the advent of the Archbishop Hanna Center for Boys, named in honor of Mitty's predecessor.

A rigorous test of the feasibility of such an undertaking was made during a pilot plan in a single cottage in the residential area of Menlo Park, a town 40 miles south of San Francisco. There in 1945, a skilled staff began rebuilding the lives of boys by giving them understanding and love, counsel and discipline, a sense of responsibility and initiative, and respect for themselves and their fellow human beings. Father James Barry was appointed the first director of the pilot project, and he was later replaced by Father Thomas Regan.

A group of Catholic laymen closely followed the pilot project and raised the funds to build a permanent home for the Center. After viewing more than 70 potential sites, the former Morris Ranch in Sonoma County's scenic Valley of the Moon, 35 miles north of San Francisco, was chosen. In September of 1948, 10,000 people gathered for the groundbreaking ceremony. Construction was completed in December of 1949, and that month, Father O'Connor, Father Regan and social worker John J. Guillaumin, along with 25 boys, moved from Menlo Park to their new home in Sonoma. A small but dedicated lay staff and five Sisters of St. Francis were awaiting their arrival.

The new facility consisted of a chapel, three cottages, an office, a dining room, a gymnasium, a swimming pool, a convent and four classrooms.

Because of increasing demand for enrollment there was a need for more living space. In 1954 three more cottages were built. Construction of these cottages was provided by free labor from the San Francisco building trades. At that time, Hanna Center housed 120 boys, consisting of private placements and wards of the courts. There were 20 boys and two counselors assigned to each cottage.

In 1955, further additions to the campus included four classrooms, a wood shop, a trade school, a dental clinic and an infirmary. The Kearney Auditorium was completed in 1957.

Father O'Connor served as Hanna Boys Center's director until October of 1972, when Father James E. Pulskamp was named his successor. Father Pulskamp was appointed chancellor of the Santa Rosa Diocese in January of 1984, and Father John Crews became director in July of that year. Under the leadership of Father Crews, two new group homes were added to the campus. These homes were dedicated and named in memory of the two founders of the Center, Monsignor Flanagan and Father O'Connor. In July of 1990, the Sisters of St. Francis retired and returned to their motherhouse in Milwaukee; the convent was converted to a cottage for 11 additional boys.

After more than 50 years of success in providing a temporary home for more than 2,700 needy and troubled boys, Hanna Boys Center continues to provide a safe, healing environment that remains constant to the Christian values upon which it was founded.

The stories of these boys, along with the highlights of the vision, dedication and energy of the staff, donors and volunteers, are captured in the pages of this book.

Father Flanagan with boys.

CHAPTER 1

Origins and Formation

Menlo Park

Reminiscing, Archbishop John J. Mitty recalled that it was Monsignor William J. Flanagan, director of Catholic Charities in San Francisco, and his assistant, Father William O'Connor, who were the first to recognize the plight of "the forgotten boy"—the youngster for whose care the "Archbishop Hanna Center for Boys" came into being. In 1944 Father O'Connor read a survey which showed alarming numbers of incidents of juvenile delinquency during World War II. The 13-county study showed a marked increase in the numbers of boys from broken homes; those affected by the moral let-down of the war years; the victims of parental neglect and questionable environment. Boys were running loose on the streets, with no one to tend them, the survey found.

The two priests laid the problem before Archbishop Mitty: in the stream of underprivileged youngsters coming to them every day for help, there seemed to be one type of boy in particular whose needs were not being met. He was a complex being, this bright-eyed youngster. Without enough supervision, structure, or consistency, and with too much time on his hands, he lacked positive direction in his life.

Too frequently, he had been turning down the wrong road—a costly road for him and society. Something had to be done. It would take love,

The first group of boys enrolled at Hanna Boys Center, Menlo Park, 1945.

Left to right: Ed (Mousie) Flynn, Russell (Sparky) Hintz, Donald Casey, John Rachal, Perry Arganbright, Terry Lagomarsino and Joseph (Poncho) Zuniga.

understanding, patience, and above all, a home—a place where he could re-whet his appetite for wholesome living—a place where he would feel wanted.

The realization of such a home became the dream of the three men.

Archbishop Mitty decided to finance the establishment of a small experimental center at Menlo Park, California. He named the demonstration unit after his predecessor, the late Most Reverend Edward J. Hanna, who was equally devoted to the cause of homeless and neglected youths.

In a small cottage in the heart of Menlo Park's residential area, the program envisioned by the three men was to undergo the most rigorous tests. The skilled, sympathetic staff—consisting of a priest, a social worker, a psychiatrist, and two house parents—began working with methods which incorporated caring, structure and consistency. They gave their charges love and understanding, and encouraged self-discipline, initiative, a sense of responsibility, and respect for the rights of others.

There were successes and heart-breaking failures during those first months, but after two years, during which the program was constantly refined, the Center came to justify its founders' highest hopes. The dream was now a tested and proven way of building good citizens.

COURTESY OF JACK PICCOLI

Jack Piccoli shows his swing.

Menlo Park House.

Life at Menlo Park

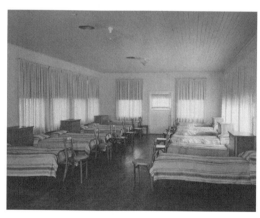

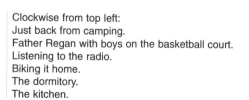

Clockwise from top left:
Just back from camping.
Father Regan with boys on the basketball court.
Listening to the radio.
Biking it home.
The dormitory.
The kitchen.

Monsignor William Flanagan, *founder*

A co-founder of the Hanna Boys Center, Monsignor William Flanagan (1902-1994) offered aid during his career not only to the Center's boys, but also to needy persons of every age and kind.

Born in San Francisco on July 16, 1902, William was the third of four children born to Margaret and Patrick Flanagan, both Irish immigrants. Patrick worked for Southern Pacific railroad while raising his family in a house he had built on the corner of 24th and Alabama Streets.

William attended the Sister of Mary and Christian Brothers parish schools, and after finishing the ninth grade at St. Peter's Grammar School, he entered St. Patrick's Seminary in Menlo Park in 1917. Archbishop Hanna ordained him on June 16, 1920, in San Francisco's St. Mary's Cathedral. His first ministry was at Our Lady of Mt. Carmel in Redwood City, where he served as associate pastor from 1928 - 1933.

During his tenure at Our Lady of Mt. Carmel, the young priest showed an aptitude for social work, and in 1933 was sent to study at the New York School of Social Work (later the Columbia University School of Social Work), where he earned his master's degree in 1934. He would also receive an honorary law degree from the University of San Francisco in 1957.

Upon his return to the Bay Area and the archdiocese, Father Flanagan put his learning to good use. He began working for Catholic Charities, then a small organization with a staff of nine; during his 24-year tenure there, he helped the organization blossom to a staff of over 100. In 1943 Father Flanagan was appointed director of the organization; that same year, his value to the church and community was recognized when Pope Pius XII appointed him a domestic prelate with the title of monsignor.

In 1944, while serving as director of Catholic Charities, Monsignor Flanagan was approached by Archbishop John Mitty and charged with the task of finding a home for "orphaned" and rejected boys. Working with Father William O'Connor, Monsignor Flanagan established the Hanna Boys Center's Menlo Park campus, which opened in 1945. As a Hanna Center pioneer, Monsignor Flanagan was involved not only in following the pilot project, but also in raising funds to establish the Sonoma campus.

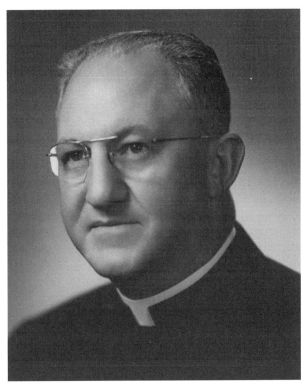

Monsignor William Flanagan

In addition to founding Hanna Center, Monsignor Flanagan also helped establish day care centers for working mothers and institutions and clinics for the aged. From 1944 to 1951, Monsignor Flanagan ran the Boys Club on Fell Street in San Francisco, which, like Hanna Center, offered support to needy youths.

While continuing to lead Catholic Charities, in 1951 Monsignor Flanagan was sent to St. Philip's Church to succeed the recently deceased Father Cantillon as the pastor. In 1957 he was named pastor of the Holy Names Church in the Sunset District of San Francisco, where he faced the challenge of building a new church. His quiet leadership and friendly manner soon inspired the parish to erect a large and modern church on the corner of 39th and Lawton Streets.

In 1978, Monsignor Flanagan retired, serving as Pastor Emeritus of Holy Names church until his death on December 29, 1994. The parishes he served, as well as the Hanna Center, continue to remember his gentlemanly demeanor, quiet leadership, and dedication.

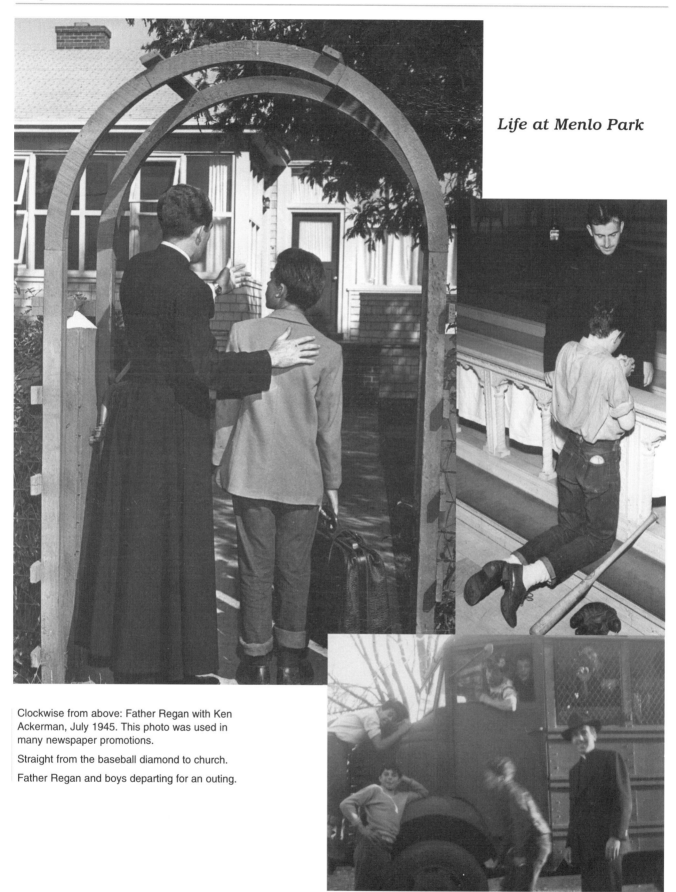

Life at Menlo Park

Clockwise from above: Father Regan with Ken Ackerman, July 1945. This photo was used in many newspaper promotions.

Straight from the baseball diamond to church.

Father Regan and boys departing for an outing.

Father Thomas Francis Regan, *associate director*

Father Thomas Regan worked as priest, social worker, recreation planner and public relations representative while serving as advocate for the boys and the Hanna Center program at Menlo Park. He continued these roles when he moved with the boys to the new campus in Sonoma Valley in 1949, where he added new duties to his self-proclaimed job description—"head wrangler and Jeep driver." Father Regan earned the reputation as one of the more colorful and energetic members of the newly formed staff of Hanna Center.

Thomas Francis Regan was born in San Francisco to Daniel and Julia Fitzpatrick Regan, both immigrants from County Cork, Ireland, on December 23, 1915. The youngest of five children, Thomas "Red" Regan attended Farragut Grammar School, from which he graduated in 1929. He attended St. Ignatius High School from 1929 until 1933, then entered St. Joseph's College in Mountain View, where he received his degree in 1935. He spent the next six years at St. Patrick's Seminary in Menlo Park, and was ordained at St. Mary's Cathedral on June 7, 1941.

Father Regan's first assignment was as assistant pastor at St. Paul's Church in San Francisco. He was then assigned to the Catholic University in Washington, D.C., from which he received a master's degree in social work in 1945.

Father Regan began working at Hanna Center in 1945 at the Center's pilot site in Menlo Park. He worked feverishly to spread the message of the success of the pilot program and to obtain public support for its expansion. In 1949 he assisted Father William O'Connor in

establishing the Center's permanent home in the Sonoma Valley, and served as assistant director to Father O'Connor there until 1958.

Father Regan was a man of action who enjoyed sharing activities with the boys. He preferred working on the ranch with the boys and animals to working at a desk in his office. He was famous for "thrilling" boys while driving his Jeep all over campus. "The fact that there weren't many roads back then didn't bother him, he drove through the fields and over the hills wherever he wanted," remembered Mrs. Ann Healy, the first (and still) executive secretary at the Center. He liked to address the boys as "hamburgers," as in, "What

are you hamburgers doing?" Many of the boys remember Father Regan as "a 'fun-loving guy' who loved just being with us."

In 1958, Father Regan was appointed director of Catholic Social Services of San Mateo County and remained there until 1963. He was appointed pastor of Our Lady of the Pillar Church and Coastside Missions in Half Moon Bay, where he worked until December of 1965, when he became pastor of St. Patrick's Church in San Jose.

Father Regan was then appointed pastor of St. Phillip's Church in 1969 and remained there until his retirement in1991; that same year, a celebration in honor of the 50th anniversary of his ordination into the priesthood was held in San Francisco and was attended by over 400 people. Father Regan continued to live in San Francisco until his death on May 13, 1993.

ORIE DAMEWOOD

Far left: Father Regan with Mike.

Above right: Father Thomas Francis Regan.

Below: Father Regan with his famous Jeep. No one was safe. Counselor John Woody is the bus driver.

The Campaign

A small group of Catholic community members had followed the experiment at Menlo Park with keen interest. When the time came, it was this group that banded together to raise the funds needed to bring Hanna Boys Center within reach of countless more "forgotten boys."

Top leaders of San Francisco and Marin Counties met in August of 1946 to complete plans for the approaching fund-raising appeal. Archbishop Mitty was the principal speaker.

"We are asking your help in a task that has proven itself to be a vital necessity," the Archbishop said. "For 18 months we operated a small center in Menlo Park to determine how many boys would benefit, and how many were in need.

"Now we know the facts," he reported. "Boys are being turned away daily—boys who, if given a good Catholic home environment, will become community assets rather than permanent liabilities."

Enthusiasm for the appeal was contagious. Campaign committees

Checking the campus model. Left to right: Jean Bertain, Father Flanagan, David Barry, Archbishop Mitty, Edwin McInnis, Andrew Welch, Vincent Compagno and Father O'Connor.

Opposite: Full-page campaign ad that appeared in the San Francisco Chronicle, November 28, 1946.

Good Citizens

....YOU CAN HELP TO BUILD THEM

MOST REV. EDWARD J. HANNA, D.D., 1860-1944
THE CHARACTER OF THIS GREAT MAN IS OUR INSPIRATION FOR BUILDING CHARACTER IN COUNTLESS BOYS

Here is your opportunity — YOUR OPPORTUNITY — to participate individually, personally, wholeheartedly, in one of the grandest, most thrilling plans ever started for the underprivileged kids of the Bay Area.

No monument of cold and silent stone—this great memorial to a great man, to which you are asked to give your dollars. Instead, your gift will grow into the glad voices of boys—fellows who somehow got the tough breaks and deserve better, fellows who are getting a new chance to grow up straight and tall in body and spirit, fellows like you and me, and our children, citizens and potential citizens, able to stand firm in a world where standing firm is so vitally necessary.

The idea behind the Archbishop Hanna Center for Boys has been pre-tested these eighteen months in the Hanna Center in Menlo Park. Successful, yes—but only 24 boys can be helped at one time. With your dollars the new, permanent Archbishop Hanna Center for Boys will build 125 stalwart citizens at one time. With your dollars will be built richer, fuller lives.

Again it is repeated — here is YOUR OPPORTUNITY. Your thoughts, your prayers and $975,000 are needed. Every contribution of yourself will be built into this memorial center and into the character of a boy. Make today your red letter day— add your part to the memorial now!

ARCHBISHOP HANNA CENTER FOR BOYS

Campaign Headquarters   Palace Hotel   EXbrook 3618

Capital Funds Campaign Committee

Most Reverend John J. Mitty, D. D., *Honorary Chairman*
Vincent I. Compagno, *Chairman*
Mrs. Edmund I. Morrissey, *Vice-Chairman*
Mrs. Harold A. Berliner, *Parish Solicitation Division Chairman*
John F. Brooke, *Founders' Division Chairman*

"On behalf of the Directors of the California Jockey Club I urge you to heed this call for your personal help. You can have a hand in creating an institution of lasting good for the present and coming generations. Let's all do our part—and more."

WILLIAM P. KYNE
General Manager
California Jockey Club, Incorporated.

This page contributed by the California Jockey Club, Incorporated (Bay Meadows Race Course)

sprang up in every county of the archdiocese, with volunteers anxious to carry the story of Hanna Boys Center to every citizen in their communities. Vincent Compagno was appointed campaign chairman and Mrs. Edmund J. Morrissey accepted the post of vice-chairman. Bay Area chairmen were also appointed: Chauncey Tramutolo for San Francisco; Guy Ciocca for Marin; Martin Flynn for San Mateo; and John Hayes for Santa Clara. Joseph Murphy served as chairman for Alameda County, while Joseph E. Kelleher chaired the Contra Costa County effort.

Chairmen for seven other counties opening their fund-raising drives on September 16, 1946, were: in Mendocino County, Mrs. W. C. Peters and James Adriani; in Lake County, John Brady; in Napa County, Jean V. Bertain and Francis Frisch; in San Joaquin County, Al Silvani and Henry A. Jopp; in Solano County, Thomas O'Dea; in Sonoma County, Joseph Lombardi; and in Stanislaus County, Ray Lewis. They set themselves a campaign goal of $975,000—"an impossible amount," said some. The mobilization was on.

Archbishop Mitty, Monsignor Flanagan, and Father O'Connor traveled to every corner of the archdiocese to speak before meetings of volunteers for the Center's campaign and local civic groups. The press caught the spirit of the drive, and a torrent of print and radio publicity gave the appeal's importance top priority in the news of the day. Pledge cards were filled out in homes, on street corners, in office buildings, and union halls—anywhere that a citizen could be stopped long enough to be told the story of "a forgotten boy."

Lights burned late those nights in the homes of volunteer committee members at campaign headquarters. There was something that made this campaign different from other appeals. Maybe it was the leadership. Perhaps the recent world war had an effect. Then again, it might have been just one image—that of a small boy in need.

Above: Father Flanagan on the radio with Chester McPhee, 1946.

Top right: At the campaign headquarters in San Francisco.

Bottom right: Victory luncheon at the Fairmont Hotel, December 20, 1946.

Among those backing the appeal was California Governor Earl Warren, who said: "There never has been a time when it is more necessary for all groups to give their best efforts for the protection of youth of California. The wholesome futures of our youngsters are a tremendous responsibility."

The San Francisco Board of Supervisors passed a resolution endorsing the appeal which stated, "Recognizing the importance and urgency of the appeal, the board of supervisors wholeheartedly endorses the campaign, and urges all citizens of San Francisco to give their generous support ... ."

Alameda County chairman Joseph Murphy praised the work of the volunteers and donors: "I wish to thank every person participating in this great drive," he said. "Each is entitled to a large measure of satisfaction in the knowledge that he is helping to build what will be one of the nation's outstanding centers for the care of homeless, unwanted and neglected boys."

On December 20, 1946, it was all over. The final figure was announced—$1,351,000—well over the goal. Adjusted for inflation, this figure equals more than $11 million in 1999 dollars—a remarkable achievement.

The dream was coming closer to reality.

ORIE DAMEWOOD

Archbishop Edward J. Hanna

The Most Reverend Edward J. Hanna, D.D.

The Archbishop Hanna Center for Boys was built and named in the memory of the Most Reverend Edward J. Hanna, D. D., who served as the Archbishop of San Francisco for 20 years.

Both of Archbishop Hanna's parents were immigrants from Ulster, Ireland, who settled in Rochester, New York. Born July 21, 1860, Edward Hanna was the oldest child in a family of three boys and three girls. His father was a cooper who made wooden barrels for the flour industry in

Rochester. Edward was educated at St. Patrick's Academy and Rochester High School, where he was valedictorian of his class. After graduation he entered the seminary at the North American College in Rome and was ordained to the priesthood in 1885. He continued his studies at the Athenaeum of the Urban College in Rome, where he received his degree of Doctor of Sacred Theology in 1886. After teaching one year at the Urban College, Father Hanna returned to the United States.

Father Hanna was assigned as an instructor at St. Bernard's Seminary in Rochester and in 1893 was appointed to the chair of Dogmatic Theology, a post he filled with distinction for almost 20 years. While serving as professor of theology, Father Hanna also worked in the diocese of St. Patrick's Cathedral, where he developed a particular interest in working with the Italian community. Sociable and sympathetic by nature, the amiable young priest became the friend of the layman. He was elected to the board of the Rochester Society for the Prevention of Cruelty to Children, helped impoverished immigrant families secure jobs and obtain legal assistance, and he helped with financial assistance when they were in need.

In 1912 Father Hanna was consecrated a bishop and assigned as Auxiliary Bishop of San Francisco. He was appointed Archbishop of San Francisco May 18, 1915, after the death of his predecessor, Archbishop Patrick J. Riordan.

During his years of service Archbishop Hanna established or expanded the facilities of 120 parishes. The building and development of Catholic schools was one of his characteristic works. He took a special interest in charitable projects and founded the Little Children's Aid and the Associated Catholic Charities. Bishop Thomas Connolly said of him, "Archbishop Hanna was in spirit and bearing ever the simple, wholehearted, kindly priest of God. He knew no distinction between the socially elite and the humblest waif of the streets."

While serving in San Francisco, Archbishop Hanna showed an active interest in community affairs. In 1913, he was appointed a member of the California Immigration and Housing Commission. In 1921 he was successful in arbitrating a strike in the building trades and was named chairman of San Francisco's impartial wage board. He was chairman of the State Committee on Unemployment (1931) and the State Emergency Committee (1933). He was a member of the National Citizens' Committee of Welfare and Relief Mobilization (1932).

California Governor James Rolph, Jr. asked Archbishop Hanna to intervene in agricultural laborers' disputes in the San Joaquin Valley in 1933. In 1934, President Franklin D. Roosevelt named him to the chairmanship of the National Longshoremen's Arbitration Board, which was able to break a strike deadlock. As chairman of the Administrative Board of the National Catholic Welfare Council from 1919 through 1935, he was the chief spokesman of the American Catholic hierarchy on matters of public concern.

Archbishop Hanna received many honors during his lifetime. The King of Italy made him a Commander of the Order of the Crown of Italy in 1922 because of his longstanding solicitude for Italian immigrants. In 1931, the University of California, citing him as a "friend of mankind," awarded him an honorary doctor of laws. He also received, that year, the American Hebrew Medal for promoting good will between Christians and Jews.

Retiring in 1935, the archbishop returned to Rome and celebrated his golden jubilee of priesthood in the Eternal City. He remained in Rome until his death on July 10, 1944. Bishop Connolly eulogized him by declaring, "His faith in human nature never diminished. His hope in the future never faltered. There never was a tone of pessimism in his public utterances. He always realized that the sun was shining behind the darkest cloud. His word was cheer and joy to all who heard it. His aims were the aims of faith." The archbishop's body was returned to San Francisco in 1947 for final burial at Holy Cross Cemetery.

His successor as Archbishop of San Francisco, Archbishop John J. Mitty, chose to honor Archbishop Hanna by dedicating Hanna Boys Center in his name. The motto of Archbishop Hanna's life, "May Christ Reign," is remembered and actualized through the work and success of Hanna Boys Center.

Site Selection

The search for a suitable site for construction of the new Center exemplifies the unselfish devotion the newly elected members of the board of directors had for their tasks. The site committee members, men who had a knowledge of land values and the legal technicalities involved in purchasing real estate, left their busy offices to make on-the-spot examinations of more than 70 different parcels of land in various sections of Northern California. John W. Carey, executive secretary of the Center, was in charge of investigating all potential sites, along with a committee of more than 50 real estate brokers, engineers, architects, appraisers and bankers.

For a time it looked like the Center would be built on property in Danville. But the committee's final choice—for reasons of climate, terrain, proximity to utilities and transportation, natural beauty, and the friendliness of the community—was a ranch comprised of 157 acres of rolling green countryside in the Sonoma Valley.

The ranch belonged to Mr. and Mrs. J. B. Morris and dated back to the early 1850s, when the family settled in Sonoma Valley. Henry Morris had been a teacher at the old Cumberland College in Sonoma.

Future site of Hanna Boys Center in Sonoma Valley. This 1887 view looks northwest from the top of the train depot at El Verano.

Right: Dinner at Sonoma Mission Inn announcing the purchase of the property.

Left to right: Joseph Lombardi, Father Flanagan, Archbishop Mitty and John Lounibos.

His son, J. B. Morris, celebrated his 90th birthday while living on the ranch. J. B.'s son, James, last owner of the ranch, was a successful sugar broker in Colorado, who left Sonoma years prior to the sale.

Mr. J. B. Morris consented very reluctantly to the sale and only for the specific use of Hanna Boys Center. He could have obtained a much higher price from outside interests, but due to the length of time the property had been in the family, he had become very attached to it, and he felt that this charitable gesture would be a fitting memorial to his family.

The property, purchased for $75,000, included machinery, tools and equipment, and stock. Sixty acres of the land were described as level, with the balance as pasture, affording a magnificent view of the Sonoma Valley. About 35 acres were planted with assorted fruit trees, and the property contained a dairy and a herd of Guernsey cows.

Archbishop Mitty announced the purchase of the property on September 16, 1947, at a dinner held at the Sonoma Mission Inn. As principal speaker of the evening, his address was broadcast on radio station KSRO. "The problem of youth is the most pressing and important problem confronting the nation and the world today," stated the Archbishop. "There are hundreds of youngsters, neglected or abandoned by their parents, who feel very confused, insecure and unwanted. Can we ignore these pitiful youngsters? Are we not, in truth, our brother's keeper?"

ORIE DAMEWOOD

He then told of the proving ground at Menlo Park which had operated so successfully. Limited facilities at Menlo Park made the present plan for the new Center imperative, so that greater good might be accomplished. "It will be an outstanding piccc of architecture of which the people of Sonoma County will be proud," said Archbishop Mitty.

Above: Archbishop Mitty announcing the purchase of the Morris Ranch on KSRO radio, September 16, 1946.

Left: Location map

"The Boy"

ORIE DAMEWOOD

Mrs. J. B. Morris of Denver, whose husband, J. Bertrand Morris, was born on the ranch which now is Hanna Center property, donated the statue to Hanna Center in memory of her husband. The inscription on the front of the statue reads: "IN MEMORY OF J. BERTRAND MORRIS WHO OWNED THIS RANCH AND LIVED HERE AS A BOY." Mr. Morris was born on April 9, 1884. He moved to Denver in 1907, where he was president of the J. B. Morris Company, a sugar brokerage. He died October 16, 1965.

The statue, located opposite the Administration Building, is called "The Boy." Sculpted by James O. Farley, it is 48 inches high, resting on a three-foot base, and weighs 200 pounds. Fabricated in Mexico, the statue is hollow and cast in antique copper bronze.

The Most Reverend Leo T. Maher, Bishop of Santa Rosa, dedicated the statue in a ceremony on June 18, 1967. Mrs. Morris and her son, as well as Monsignor William O'Connor and Hanna board of directors chairman John Lounibos, attended the ceremony. Bishop Maher commented that the statue was a fitting memorial to Mr. Morris—a symbol of values and ideals.

The artist wanted to depict a boy with a suitcase, in need of help, arriving at the Center. Since 1967 "The Boy" has been a part of numerous photographic opportunities and a point of interest on campus tours conducted by the boys. The statue has been used as a logo on letterheads, public announcements and promotions as a symbol of a "troubled boy" seeking hope at Hanna Boys Center.

Left: A Hanna boy poses with "The Boy" statue.

Above: Rear view of the statue before bronzing.

The Sisters of St. Francis

Mother Bartholomew, Father Flanagan and Sister Grace review the scale model of Hanna Boys Center, September, 1948.

Right: Mother Bartholomew, surrounded by (from left): Sister Theophane, Sister Clare, Sister Celise, Sister Grace, Father Doyle, Sister Maxelinda and Sister Bernadette, September, 1949.

As the fundraising campaign and site search progressed, so, too, did plans for the foundation of a school at the Center. Monsignor O'Connor began enquiring as to whether there might be an order of nuns devoted to teaching and education, whose members might serve as instructors at Hanna. In 1946, at a meeting in Chicago, Father O'Connor mentioned his search to other priests—one of whom highly recommended the Sisters of St. Francis of Assisi, whose motherhouse was in Milwaukee.

The religious order traced its roots back to 1849, when a small group of secular men and women, who were members of the third order of St. Francis of Assisi, left Ettenbeuren, Bavaria, to sail to North America, with the goal of becoming missionaries. They arrived in Wisconsin and settled on a site along the shores of Lake Michigan. The women in this group were the pioneers in establishing the Order of the Sisters of St. Francis of Assisi of Penance and Charity.

Since its inception, the order had established an excellent reputation. The sisters' work as educators—as well as their expertise in

Mother Mary Bartholomew, *superior, teacher*

The person most responsible for the Sisters of St. Francis of Assisi coming to Hanna Boys Center was certainly Mother Mary Bartholomew. Because of her great love for the underprivileged, Mother Bartholomew's heart and mind were drawn to the concept of Hanna when she first heard of it from Monsignor Flanagan. She promised that by the time the school was built, she would send five sisters to teach there. And Mother Bartholomew had never been known to make a promise she did not keep.

She was born in Paris, Wisconsin, and even as a young child exhibited leadership qualities. These qualities remained with her as she entered the Order of St. Francis in 1897 at the early age of 15. She received her bachelor of arts degree from DePaul University in Chicago, and in the early years taught in Illinois and Wisconsin.

In 1930, Mother Bartholomew became assistant to the mother general and two years later, with the help of other sisters, established St. Clare's College, now known as Cardinal Stritch University. In 1933, she journeyed to China to visit the missions the community had established; during her several months there, she became acquainted with customs and manners of Chinese life—information that served her well later, when she directed the Chinese missions. In July of 1937, Mother Bartholomew became the 11th superior-general of the St. Francis community. She served for 12 years that were filled with multiple accomplishments. Often Mother Bartholomew was called a risk taker; she would smile at that and say she'd rather believe it was having deep faith.

In 1955, when she came to Hanna Boys Center as superior of the house and a part-time teacher, Mother Bartholomew continued to encourage and inspire. She believed in hard work, but also knew the value of relaxation. She loved telling stories and enjoyed hearing the stories of others, especially those enriched with humor. Mother Bartholomew had a deep love for all the students and they were in her prayers daily. Her parting words, each morning, to the sisters as they'd leave for their classrooms was always, "Be good to the boys."

Mother Bartholomew was a woman of wisdom, a woman of deep faith. She enjoyed life and often said she hoped to live to be 100. She almost got her wish. Mother died at the age of 99 on December 12, 1981.

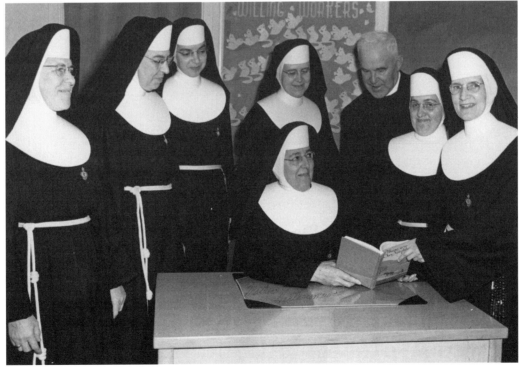

THE STAGGS PHOTOGRAPHY

special education—were widely known, not only in parish schools, but also in specialized areas at St. John's School for the Deaf and St. Aemillian's Orphanage.

In August of 1946, Mother Mary Bartholomew, who headed the order in Milwaukee, received a letter from Monsignor William Flanagan. In it was a request for a group of sisters to come to California to staff a school that had not yet been built. Mother Bartholomew's first reaction was that she did not have any sisters available to send. However, the idea of a school for underprivileged and neglected boys intrigued her. She granted Monsignor Flanagan's request to come to the motherhouse in Milwaukee to discuss the idea with her. At that meeting, Mother Bartholomew became convinced that Hanna Center was indeed a suitable undertaking for the Sisters of Saint Francis.

Sister Edwardine works with a Hanna student.

Hopes were high that a teaching staff would arrive by the time the school and cottages were built. In May of 1947, Mother Bartholomew sent the news that she could send five sisters for the educational program at the new Hanna Boys Center. In one of her letters to Monsignor Flanagan, she wrote, "I am deeply interested in the project and as eager as you are to get started. You may rest assured we shall send you well-trained personnel. Already, I am gradually selecting the sisters in order to give them the opportunity to take special courses for the work, if needed."

A little less than a year after writing that letter, Mother Bartholomew found herself among the crowd at the groundbreaking ceremony for Hanna Boys Center, witnessing the beginning of a dream come true. Although there were no buildings yet on the site where the Sisters of St. Francis would begin a new work, she felt grateful that her sisters would be a major part of this dream.

Groundbreaking

September 19, 1948—State Highway Patrol officers said over 10,000 people were present for the impressive groundbreaking ceremonies that warm summer day. They had come from every county of the archdiocese—some from more distant cities.

There were no buildings to be seen—just gently sloping hills, groves of oak and eucalyptus trees, a blue sky, and in the distance, a small platform on which was seated a welcoming committee of civic leaders from the Sonoma Valley and the speakers of the day.

Radio station KSRO broadcast the entire program. The audience heard the singing voices of nearly a thousand parochial school children, the opening message of Board Chairman Edward McInnis, and the warm welcome to Hanna Center expressed by John Lounibos of Petaluma, who spoke on behalf of Sonoma County.

Hanna Boys Center groundbreaking, September 19, 1948. Left to right: Father Regan, Archbishop Mitty, Father John Barry, Ken Ackerman (Hanna student with shovel), Father Flanagan, Henri Maysonnave and Monsignor Sheen.

ORIE DAMEWOOD

Left: Monsignor Sheen giving the address at the groundbreaking ceremony. Irene Dunne (left) introduced him.

Above: Monsignor Sheen (right) delivers holy water sent by Pope Pius XII to Archbishop Mitty.

Below: View of the crowd at the groundbreaking celebration. The Highway Patrol estimated that 10,000 people attended.

John J. Guillaumin, assistant director

John Guillaumin joined the staff of Hanna Boys Center in January of 1945. He served as Assistant Director until his retirement on January 19, 1977.

Because he was part of a small staff when the Sonoma campus of Hanna Center first opened, Mr. Guillaumin did a little bit of everything in the office—from fund-raising to coordinating enrollment of boys—in addition to counseling and disciplining them. On Saturdays he could be seen with a mop and a bucket, washing the floors of the administration building. He was particularly close to Father O'Connor, and was known for his sense of humor and clowning with Father Regan.

Mr. Guillaumin attended Our Lady of Sorrows grammar school in Detroit, Michigan; Assumption College High School in Canada; and was a graduate of Sacred Heart College in Detroit, where he earned his B. A. He also attended Mount St. Mary's College in Cincinnati, Ohio. He earned his degree in social work from the University of Detroit and Wayne University. Prior to working at Hanna, Mr. Guillaumin served as director of vocational education for five years at Boys Republic in Farmington, Michigan. Mr. Guillaumin and his wife, Anne, had a son, John, and two daughters, Joan and Elizabeth.

Mr. Guillaumin was honored by Pope John in February of 1963 with the Pro Ecclesia et Pontifice Medal. This decoration ("For Church and Pontiff") is given in recognition of service to the church and the papacy. Boys and staff were saddened by his death on January 6, 1978. A memorial Mass in the Hanna chapel was concelebrated by Monsignor O'Connor, Father Pulskamp, Monsignor William J. Flanagan, Monsignor John O'Hare, Father Thomas Regan and Father Richard Grever. Boys and staff attended the Mass.

Above: John Guillauman distributing gifts to boys at Christmas time.

Monsignor Fulton J. Sheen was there. He had journeyed to Sonoma from Washington, D.C., to make the main address. He was introduced by his good friend, actress Irene Dunne, who had flown up from Hollywood. Monsignor Sheen spoke of the need for training the nation's youth: "Education is not enough. The will and the character must be trained."

Monsignor Sheen's magnificent address was followed by Archbishop Mitty's own expression of gratitude to those present for their unflagging interest in a great humanitarian undertaking. Archbishop Mitty reviewed the history of the project and praised the enthusiasm of Monsignor Flanagan and Father O'Connor, describing their efforts as a noble work—"the heritage of happy youth, love and solicitation for the welfare of these boys."

Then came the climax. A youngster from the Center sank a gold shovel into the soft earth. As Archbishop Mitty prepared to bless the ground, the audience, sensing the significance of the moment, broke through the rope barriers, and all but swept members of the official party off their feet with their enthusiasm.

Ground had been broken. The next day construction would begin.

Construction

Throughout the fall of 1948, bulldozers and tractors tore away at the hills. Soon the concrete forms were in place, and red-leaded steel beams shot up from the ground. A deep well tapped an unlimited supply of fresh water, and power lines brought in the necessary electricity.

Left untouched was the acreage across Arnold Drive where an orchard and a small poultry operation formed the nucleus of a farm. Here, the boys would learn the rudiments of agriculture and also help supply their own tables with meat, vegetables, and fresh fruit.

All through this period the city and county officials of Sonoma consulted with Hanna Center committee members, lending them generous cooperation, counsel, and advice as the building program progressed. Costs had soared since the original $975,000 campaign goal had been

Mr. J. F. Thurber (left) with Father O'Connor (center) and Father Flanagan (right) at the construction site.

Opposite right: The gymnasium, as viewed from the front access road.

Center: The gymnasium.

Bottom: One of the boys' cottages.

set in 1946, and to build the Center as first planned would now cost more than the amount raised. Construction of three of the Center's six residential cottages had to be postponed temporarily.

Even though the plans had long since been completed, the building committee continued to meet regularly in an effort to cut costs without reducing the scope of the project or the spirit of the program. Committee members, meeting with the board of directors, made periodic visits to check on construction progress, and then returned to San Francisco to assign themselves new tasks and more responsibilities.

On several occasions the youngsters from Menlo Park Center visited their new home to stare excitedly at the gymnasium, the swimming pool, and—with a little less interest—at the school. As the fall months of 1949 passed, construction was stepped up in a drive to "get the boys in by Christmas."

C. M. MERLIN JONES

ORIE DAMEWOOD

ORIE DAMEWOOD

Construction progressed to the point where five sisters of St. Francis were able to move into Loretto cottage on November 27, 1949. The following day, Father O'Connor moved into the priests' residence. Much had been accomplished since 1945—from preliminary planning to fund-raising, site selection, and construction. Only 15 months after the groundbreaking ceremony, the campus was ready for the boys to arrive. Five years of vision, dedication and work were about to culminate in an emotional welcome and another beginning.

Opposite, top: The chapel, August 19, 1949.

Bottom: The chapel and dining hall, December 5, 1949.

Right: Sculptor Ruth Cravath and Father O'Connor work on the statue above the chapel door.

Below: The interior of the chapel.

Above: Aerial view of early construction.

Below, left: A Hanna boy helps a heavy equipment operator.

Below, right: Loretto Cottage, December 5, 1949.

Ruth Cravath, artist

The beautiful works of sculptor Ruth Cravath adorn Our Lady of Fatima Chapel at Hanna Center. Ms. Cravath did a tremendous amount of work for the Center, sculpting all of the statuary within the chapel including the Our Lady of Fatima statue, the Corpus over the altar, the Madonna, Sacred Heart statue and the exquisite 14 Stations of the Cross.

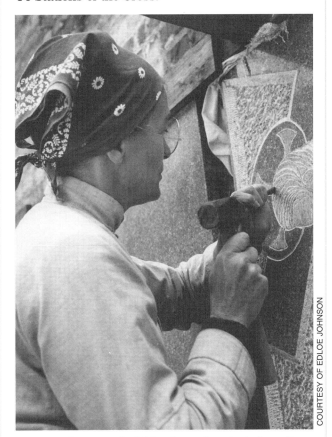

In February of 1950, when she started on the Lady of Fatima statue which adorns the façade of Hanna's chapel, she insisted that all of the boys residing at the Center, plus priests, sisters and staff members, do some chiseling on this marvelous piece of work. Mrs. Ann Healy posed as a model for Our Lady's hands for Ms. Cravath. The sculptor lived in Loretto Cottage while she was working on the statue. She completed the statue in three months, in time for the dedication of Hanna Center.

Born January 23, 1902, in Chicago, she studied art at the Chicago Art Institute and Grinnell College in Grinnell, Iowa, before coming to San Francisco in 1921. From the mid-1920s to the late

1970s, Ruth Cravath distinguished herself as a sculptor in San Francisco. She taught at the California School of Fine Arts, Mills College and Dominican College and produced numerous garden and civic sculptures before specializing in liturgical sculpture.

On April 2, 1953, Ms. Cravath made a gift to Hanna Center of a plaque of the Sacred Heart in memory of her mother. She wanted it placed at the East doorway so that the boys would be able to touch the hand of Christ as they left the chapel each morning.

"Ruth Cravath was a true friend and benefactor of Hanna Boys Center and will never be forgotten by our founders and early supporters who knew her," said Father John Crews. "Nor will she be forgotten by the scores of boys, visitors, staffers and administrators here who will be privileged to view her beautiful work down through the years," Father Crews said.

Left: Ruth Cravath at work.

Below: Detail of the third Station of the Cross by Ruth Cravath.

Al Carli, *alumnus*

As one of Hanna Center's first alumni, Al Carli has maintained close ties with teachers and staff of the Center throughout his adult life and career. Al is one of the few boys who lived in Hanna's original Menlo Park facility and who made the transition to the Sonoma campus. Consequently, Al has given first-hand accounts of life in Menlo Park, and he can compare the sparse living conditions there to the amenities of the new Center.

Al was a student who took full advantage of all aspects of Hanna life. A successful student at Hanna, Al continued that success in his education, athletic life, family life and working career. Now retired, Al continues to have fond memories of Hanna Center.

Al Carli was born June 5, 1937, in Redwood City, to parents Albert Michael Carli and Lena Cappini. He was raised by his grandmother, an elderly woman "who had little control over me," Al recalled. "Consequently I was mostly on my own."

Al's independent lifestyle changed when he was placed into Hanna Center's pilot program in Menlo Park in 1949. Sharing a house, dorm room, and dining room with 27 other boys changed his perspective.

"It was very cozy there, and we formed a tight net of boys who looked out for each other," he said. "This has always stayed with me. I learned to watch out for and to protect my family."

In December of 1949, Hanna Center moved to its new, spacious Sonoma campus—an exciting occasion for Al and his classmates.

"We were hanging out of the bus windows trying to see this new home of ours," he recalled.

"Leaving the bus, we were led to a cottage with our suitcase in hand. My cottage was Rosary Hill. Inside the cottage, we couldn't believe what we saw. Our eyes were as big as balloons. There was a living room and a recreation room and an area with tables along the wall suitable for studying or reading. 'Man oh man'—a fireplace, too!"

Al spent three years at Hanna's Sonoma campus, and then moved on to a foster home, where he was adopted by Bill and Georgia Slakey. They lived in Santa Cruz for three months before moving to Piedmont, near Oakland. Under the Slakeys' guidance Al completed three years of high school at Saint Mary's College Prep High School in Berkeley, enlisted in the Marine Corps, and then settled into a job as a warehouseman at Slakey Brothers in Oakland.

Al worked at Slakey's Oakland facility before being transferred to the Richmond warehouse, where he was sole operator of the facility. "You may see him waiting on the trade at the city counter; receiving and shipping merchandise; keeping the warehouse in order; and even keeping the coffee pot full so that his customers may enjoy a cup of coffee while their orders are being filled," said supervisor Everitt Welliver. "Al is the type of person you can rely on to give you only the type of service you expect and deserve."

Now retired and living in Union City with his fiancée, Loris Cook, Al said he remains busy keeping in touch with his four children—Anita, Bernice, Charles, and Darlene—and seven grandchildren, all living in Colorado. Al is a charter member of the Hanna Alumni Association and has served as president and in other official positions of the association. Al has also been a regular contributor to the Hanna Center's alumni newsletter— and although recovery from a 1995 back operation has been lengthy, Al said he plans to return again to the Sonoma campus to visit.

Al Carli exemplifies the positive change a boy can achieve from his participation in the program at Hanna Boys Center. When he first came to the Center, he was a boy in need of structure, supervision and attention. He fully engaged himself in the activities of the Center—especially the athletic program. Al was able to use these experiences when he moved on to play high school football, graduate from high school and succeed in the Marine Corps. He incorporated the values that he learned at the Center into his family life when raising his own children. Al has remained steadfast in his loyalty to Hanna Center ever since he was that wide-eyed little boy looking out the bus window on December 4, 1949.

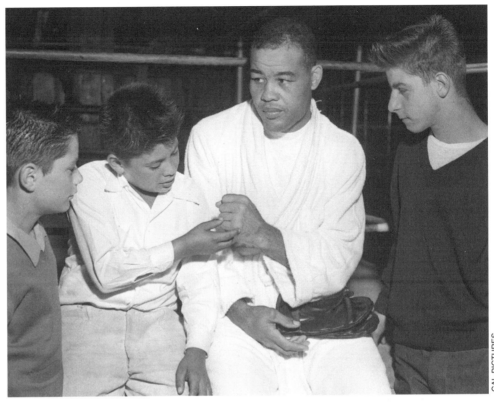

CAL-PICTURES

Opposite: 1951 Field Day. Left to right: Al Carli, Bob Carroll and Phillip Martinez.

Above: Fred Starr (left), Rudy Martinez and Al Carli (right) meet heavyweight champion Joe Louis.

Right: Al Carli (left) shares photos with Lou Ferrario, supervisor of the recreation department, during Alumni Day.

Father O'Connor with boys

CHAPTER 2

The O'Connor Years 1949–1972

Arrival

It was Sunday, December 4, 1949. Father O'Connor and the five Sisters of St. Francis who served as faculty were standing in front of the chapel at Hanna Boys Center. Twilight was beginning to silhouette the buildings against the sky. It was getting late, and the reception committee was anxiously awaiting the boys' arrival from Menlo Park.

Al Carli was one of the youngsters on the bus slowly making its way to the Valley of the Moon. He remembered it this way: "We were very excited to see this new home where we were heading. We had an old bus which we called Hurty Gurty, that probably had to make six stops because of over-heating. Consequently, when we arrived in Sonoma it was dark."

Finally, the welcoming committee spotted the huge bus swinging up the newly graveled driveway. Boys' heads crammed through the bus windows, arms waved, and there were cries of "Hi!" and "Here we come!" as the bus rolled slowly to a stop. The door of the bus swung open and 25 eager, shouting lads tried to come through the three-foot doorway three abreast.

The scene must have seemed like an excerpt from a Hollywood script as one boy came down the steps of the bus on crutches. There were embraces and greetings all around. Someone had the presence of mind to snap a few pictures to record the event.

Sister Mary Grace often recalled what happened after the boys disembarked from the bus. The sisters had wanted to help make the arrival a very special occasion, and planned a festive party, decorating the tables in the dining rooms, filling hand-decorated cups with candy and nuts. After settling into their cottages, the boys were brought down to

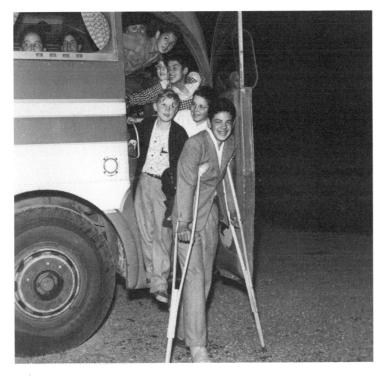

the dining room. The sisters looked for expressions of delight, but instead they saw the boys rip into the nut cups and gobble up the contents—showing little interest in fancy decorations. The meal, too, was eaten in much haste.

For entertainment, Father Regan had planned a movie, but forgot to bring it. He asked the sisters to keep the boys occupied while he went to retrieve it. Sister Mary Grace remembered attempting to teach her charges a game called "Fifty." She recalled how they cheated without a qualm. Fights broke out that carried into the hallway; those who weren't fighting gathered around yelling and cheering. Fortunately, Father O'Connor arrived and broke up the melee. It was quite an initiation for the sisters.

Despite the rowdiness, the arrival of the boys was a joyous occasion. Father O'Connor and the sisters of St. Francis finally had their boys, and the boys finally had a home. The history of Hanna Boys Center in Sonoma had begun. The work of caring, teaching and shaping the lives of young boys had been initiated with a sense of hope that would sustain the Center for the next 50 years and beyond.

Opposite: Father O'Connor greets the boys as they exit the bus at Hanna Center.

Top: Ward Jones (on crutches), Bill Sheridan (left), Neal Black, Tony Morbito (checked shirt), Elmer Ritchie and Ken Green (leaning out door).

Above: Original staff: Father O'Connor, Father Regan, John Guillaumin, Jim Healy, Ann Healy, C. Hodges, Sister Grace, Sister Clare, Sister Ferdinanda, Sister Regina, Sister Charity, Sister Madeleva, John Zek, Mario Carota, Farley Mohun, Robert Rouse, M. McLaughlin and Eileen Meroney.

Monsignor William L. O'Connor, *founder*

Monsignor William O'Connor

"There wouldn't be a Hanna Boys Center without Bill O'Connor."

So remarked the late Monsignor William J. Flanagan at a retirement dinner honoring his long time friend and close associate, Monsignor William L. O'Connor.

Appointed the first director of Hanna Boys Center in June of 1949, the then-Father O'Connor would, 23 years later, be named a Prothonotary Apostolic by Pope Paul VI, on March 22, 1972.

Monsignor O'Connor served as Hanna Center's director until 1972, when he was, at his request, reassigned as the associate director. He served in that capacity until his retirement 1984—ending 35 years as the heart and soul of Hanna Boys Center.

Monsignor Flanagan's tribute to Monsignor

O'Connor cannot be faulted. After all, it was Monsignor Flanagan and Monsignor O'Connor who in 1944 first sought to found a home for troubled and rejected boys. This was their dream, and Hanna Boys Center was the result of that dream, with Monsignor O'Connor the acknowledged chief dreambuilder. As that home began to take shape, there seems little doubt but that Monsignor Flanagan recommended Monsignor O'Connor as the logical choice to serve as the founding executive director of Hanna Boys Center.

William Lawrence O'Connor was born in San Francisco on June 6, 1907, the son of William O'Connor and Belle (Walsh) O'Connor. He received his education at St. James School in San Francisco; St. Joseph's College in Mountain View; St. Patrick's Seminar in Menlo Park; and the New York School of Social Work (Columbia University), New York City.

He began his career as a Roman Catholic priest in 1932, serving as assistant pastor at St. Rose Church in Santa Rosa, until 1934, when he was named assistant director of Catholic Social Services for the Archdiocese of San Francisco.

It was during his 15 years with Catholic Social Services that Monsignor O'Connor became deeply concerned over the number of neglected, angry— and sometimes orphaned—young boys getting into trouble at home, in school and, too often, with the law.

It was out of those concerns that he dreamed of providing a facility with a homelike atmosphere and guidance from caring and trained adults, where a boy on the wrong road could find the right path by learning moral and spiritual values, along with receiving academic and vocational training.

A deeply religious person, it was Monsignor O'Connor, while studying the initial building plans for the Center, who insisted that the chapel be placed in the center of the campus.

"It was symbolic of his belief that spiritual values are the foundation of any education and growing up," said his present-day successor, Father John Crews, following Monsignor O'Connor's death on December 30, 1991.

Mrs. Ann Healy, the Center's veteran executive secretary, to whom Monsignor O'Connor often referred as "the world's best secretary," recalls the substantial amount of time he spent in the chapel each day. The most senior member of the Hanna staff, Mrs. Healy came here late in 1949 from Boys Town, Nebraska. As Monsignor O'Connor's secretary, she perhaps knew him better than anyone.

"Actually, he was a very simple man, yet adamant about trying to instill in every boy the desire to improve and to gain from their stay at Hanna Center," Mrs. Healy said.

"He was fair, but the boys knew him as a no-nonsense disciplinarian, and he won their respect—despite their trembling whenever receiving the message 'Monsignor O'Connor would like to see you in his office.' He also earned the respect of those who worked with him. The nuns revered him. I lucked out having him for a boss," she added.

"He read the mail every day and was prompt to answer those who sought a reply. Tuesday was his day off and was when he enjoyed his favorite hobby, golf. He played regularly at the Olympic Club course in San Francisco with Monsignor Flanagan of Holy Names parish and Monsignor Clem McKenna of St. Vincent's."

Monsignor O'Connor's several voyages on tramp steamers to various ports around the world also delighted him. Monsignor Flanagan accompanied him on these "limited passenger facilities" cruises, which also afforded him ample time to pursue another favorite hobby, the voracious reading of countless "whodunit" mystery novels.

But his happiest and most comforting times were when he received a personal visit, a telephone call or a letter from one of the hundreds of boys to whom he administered during his 35 years at Hanna Boys Center—most of them thanking him and the Center staff for giving them a real chance at living happy, spiritually motivated and productive lives.

Monsignor O'Connor died peacefully in his sleep, at age 83, on December 30, 1992, at Nazareth House, a Catholic retirement home in San Rafael, where he had lived since 1988. Some of "his boys" served as pallbearers at the funeral mass held in his beloved chapel at Hanna Boys Center on January 3, 1992. Burial was in Calvary Catholic Cemetery in Santa Rosa.

The First Day of School

On Thursday, December 8th, the Feast Day of the Blessed Virgin Mary, Sisters Mary Grace, Mary Clare, Charity, Madeleva and Mary Ferdinanda moved into the Center's beautiful new convent. Though there were only five sisters, the convent contained 10 bedrooms. That in itself was a statement of hope that there would be more sisters coming as the school grew.

The following day, Friday, December 9th, the school doors of Hanna Boys Center opened for the first time to the 25 students who had arrived from the Menlo Park site. Initially there were six rooms. Five were to be used as classrooms; the sixth became a combination classroom and library. The boys were assigned to home rooms ranging from sixth to ninth grade.

The sisters were eager to start that first day of school, but not without a great deal of anxiety. They woke up to pouring rain. Boys pushed and shoved each other into puddles on their way to school, and a few fights broke out. One of the boys had a glass eye, so to annoy his teacher, he would roll it across his desk. It was apparent that for the most part, the boys did not seem eager to get down to the business of learning. To make matters worse, many books and materials were still on back order. The school was not yet completely finished, so some of the dining rooms were needed as classrooms.

Behavior on the part of the boys left much to be desired. It was evident that their problems were many. It would take experience, love and commitment to understand that each boy's feelings of fear, frustration, insecurity, anxiety and anger would sometimes explode into aggressive and hostile actions. And it was going to take the full cooperation of each staff member in order to succeed in helping these boys.

Sister Mary Grace, principal, psychologist

During her 20th year of teaching 8th grade students at Sacred Heart School in Milwaukee, Sister Mary Grace was called to the motherhouse by Mother Mary Bartholomew and informed of the decision to send her to Loyola University to earn a master's degree in psychology.

The long-range plan was then explained: Sister Mary Grace was to become the principal and, along with four other sisters, to set up an educational program for underprivileged and neglected boys in a school not yet constructed, called Hanna Boys Center in Sonoma, California.

That was over 50 years ago. Sister Mary Grace was not only the driving force in establishing a curriculum geared to the needs of these youngsters, but she also became a mentor to many young sisters who profited from her wealth of experience and understanding.

Sister Mary Grace entered the Order of the Sisters of St. Francis in 1925. Through the years, her educational background became extensive: she obtained a bachelor's degree in education from Cardinal Stritch College, and a master's degree in psychology from Loyola University in Chicago. She attended the University of San Francisco, Marquette University in Milwaukee, and the Catholic University of America in Washington, D. C., as well as Boston College. While abroad, Sister Mary Grace attended classes in Geneva, Switzerland, receiving a Certificate from L'Institute International Seminaire d'Education.

While at Hanna, Sister Mary Grace became a full-time psychologist and consultant to the staff. Her insights were invaluable to many. As principal, her door was always open to any boy who had a problem and wished to talk. She was a tremendous help to teachers, giving suggestions on how to work through difficult situations.

Sister Mary Grace left Hanna in October of 1985. She stated that the most difficult thing she had to do was retire from her work; poor health dictated her decision.

Though Sister Mary Grace's health no longer permits her to travel back to Sonoma, the place where a dream came true, she will always be remembered for the pivotal role she played in that dream when she accepted the challenge of Mother Bartholomew so long ago: "I want you to go to Hanna Boys Center and establish an educational program for underprivileged and neglected boys."

Opposite: A classroom scene.

Right: Sister Peter in class.

ORIE DAMEWOOD

The Boys' Program

The program developed by Father O'Connor, Father Regan, Assistant Director John Guillaumin, the sisters and other staff members was one that would endure in its basic form and content for the next 50 years. The program might best be described by a short synopsis taken from the back of early stationery the Center used for correspondence. It read as follows:

Sister Peter giving a history lesson.
Opposite top: Boys at the chapel.
Bottom: On the ranch.

A Boy's Life at Hanna Center

As much as we can make it so, a boy's life here is a happy one. The lad who comes to live with us in our little town in this beautiful valley could be the same boy who might be found in your home, or in the home of someone you know in your town. Usually, he is here because someone has failed him. With the help of those who support our work, we seek our objective of bringing the boy up in an atmosphere designed to be as normal and homelike as possible. Our boy is guided toward moral, mental and physical fulfillment. In the planning of his daily routine, we do our very best to lead him through his boyhood in a way which will prepare him for a manhood of honor, productiveness and responsibility.

The boy's day may include such varied activities as a visit to the chapel, his academic and trade school classes, daily chores, time on the ranch, participation in scouting and similar activities, organized athletics and time to just plain play and relax. In almost every case, he takes pride in achieving the goals set for him. Daily, he asks God's blessing for all who help him.

The goals of the program are:
- To respect the rights of others;
- To live within reasonable boundaries;
- To control inappropriate impulses;
- To accept responsibility for the consequences of behavior;
- To acquire the academic, technical, and social skills essential to be a productive member of society; and
- To respect and revere self, others, and God.

ORIE DAMEWOOD

The founders believed that the principal uniqueness and strength of Hanna Center was its foundation on religious faith, specifically, the Christian faith as embodied in the traditions, values and practices of the Roman Catholic Church. The rituals of morning and evening prayer, blessing at meals, religious instruction at school, and Sunday services were at the heart of a boy's life at the Center. Father O'Connor explained it in simple terms:

"The reason we started Hanna Center was to make Catholic boys better Catholics, and for those boys who didn't know God, to introduce them to Him."

The experiences of some of the residents during the early years of the Center illustrate how the daily routine worked to promote lasting changes in the lives of the boys. Frank Youngblood, a student in 1958 and 1959, remembers it this way: "I arrived at the Center as a troubled 15-year-old. The nuns took me to their hearts and for the first time I felt that someone cared, and finally I had a family. I have found in my adult life that the religious education I received at Hanna meant more to me than any other help I received."

George Gomes, a student from November of 1959 through June of 1962, talked about his conversion to Catholicism while at Hanna Center. "I liked religion and got good grades in that subject. I fell in love with Catholicism, and I wanted to become a Catholic and be a part of all that. I was baptized and became an altar boy. Child care worker Ken Krumdick is my godfather and administrative secretary Ann Healy is my godmother."

Many of the boys who came to the Center had difficulties at their previous schools. They found the learning environment different from what they had experienced earlier. Al Haggett, a student from 1950 through 1952, was strongly influenced by Sister Mary Peter, who "had a unique way of dealing with boys; she could get the most out of you," he said. "She brought me to an 'A' average and she convinced me that I had the smarts to succeed in school."

George Gomes added, "You really couldn't not learn in that school."

Keeping the boys busy with sports, work and other activities was a key to success in their treatment. Achieving goals in a variety of different

Top: Practicing a few chords.
Bottom: Time for a treat.

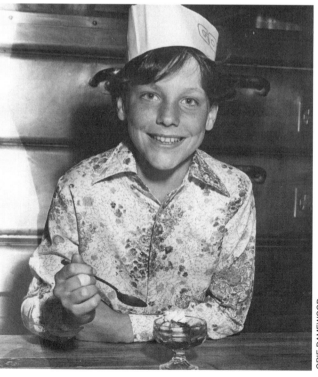

activities improved the boys' positive self-images and gave them confidence. John Benedetti, student from 1959 to 1963, summed up his experience this way: "I got involved in different things at Hanna. I was an altar boy, and I served Mass there every day for three years. I was in the choir and the band. The different jobs I had, like staff waiter and working on the ranch, were good because when I left Hanna I wasn't afraid to work."

Harry Dillon, also a student in 1956 and 1957, said: "I remember two things about Hanna Center—the staff and the work. When a boy is 15 or 16 and there is an adult in his life who cares about him, the boy knows it, he just knows it. We had a lot of caring people at Hanna, and it rubbed off on me. My first job was working on the ranch. Mr. James Joseph McKenna was the head ranch-er and he made us work hard. I remember baling hay in 110-degree heat. When I got tired of ranch work, I got a job in the kitchen making 10 cents an hour, which looked like a lot of money to me then."

ORIE DAMEWOOD

Sports provided another outlet for achieving success and building self-esteem. Thirty-four years after he graduated from Hanna, George Gomes maintains fond memories of his athletic activity at the Center. "I believe that I still hold the Center records for the 50- and 100-yard dashes and for the eight-pound shot put," he said. "I still have the ribbons; they are my prized possessions."

Instilling values in a young man is a gradual process requiring consistency and positive role modeling. The Hanna staff's success in this endeavor is illustrated by three of the Center's alumni. George Gomes said, "The people of Hanna allowed me to be me. I learned a lot about truth and honesty. The Center became the basis for my whole life, because it made me a good person."

Top: Final instructions before the game from Coach Adrian Monsano.

Bottom: George Gomes, class of '62. George and his wife of 31 years, Carolynn, have one daughter. George served in the U.S. Army with the 101st Airborne Division and had a career as a construction superintendent.

Al Haggett remembers it this way: "The dedication of the people of Hanna had a strong influence on building character. I picked up a lot from Hanna. I think I learned some values and I got a better feeling about myself."

"The values that I learned at the Center were not evident at the time I left," recalled John Benedetti. "But when they finally took hold of me, I couldn't deny them. They were there —treat people with respect, treat property and the environment with respect, leave a place a little better than you found it, the 'Golden Rule,' treat people like they are your own family, common courtesy—it all becomes a positive outlook that you use all of your life."

Education, hard work, strong body, respect for self and others, importance of family and a relationship with God— these are the values that have remained steadfast throughout the history of Hanna Boys Center, and these are the values that sustain the boys as they proceed through life and establish their careers and families.

Left: Harry Dillon, class of '57, with Irma Landier. Harry is the proud father of two daughters and is retired from the Navy, in which he served as a SEAL.

Above: Al Haggett, class of '52, with his wife, Tootka. Al has over 28 years with the San Francisco Police Department's Communications Division —911 Emergency Calling Service.

Below: John Benedetti, class of '63, a design engineer for Pacific Gas and Electric, is the father of two daughters.

Jim Healy, first athletic director

One of the original group of staff members, Jim Healy was the first athletic director of Hanna Boys Center. Understanding the importance of physical education, athletics and recreation, Jim set a standard of excellence that has come to characterize this important aspect of each boy's treatment at Hanna.

Mr. Healy was born in San Mateo, California. His father was a patent attorney and his mother was a deputy sheriff for San Mateo County. Jim attended San Mateo High School, and following the Japanese attack on Pearl Harbor he joined the Navy, serving until 1946 in the Pacific theatre. Initially in the submarine forces, he later graduated from the U.S. Divers' School in Washington, D.C., where he became one of the Navy's youngest ever master divers.

After the war he attended San Mateo College, and later graduated from San Francisco State University with bachelor's and master's degrees in physical education.

While a teacher and athletic instructor at Boys Town, Nebraska, Mr. Healy met and married Ann Rodis, a member of the Boys Town secretarial staff. Their brief honeymoon journey across the country was to Sonoma, California, where Mr. Healy had accepted Father William O'Connor's offer to become athletic director at Hanna Boys Center. Father O'Connor also quickly recruited Ann as his secretary, and Ann joined Jim on the Hanna Center staff. This husband and wife team greeted the busload of boys from the Menlo Park campus on December 4, 1949.

As the first athletic director of Hanna, Mr. Healy established physical education classes, instituted intramural sports, created inter-scholastic team competition, held boxing matches and instituted field day competitions. He was also creative in planning trips for boys to ball games and to meet famous sports personalities. He was instrumental in coordinating several professional prize fights, with the proceeds donated to Hanna.

In addition to developing Hanna Boys Center's athletic curriculum, Mr. Healy was the boys' role model for physical fitness and good sportsmanship. A fine athlete himself, he participated in

Left: James Edward Healy.

Below: A few pointers in shooting.

athletic events until his unfortunate death. He participated in the Bay to Breakers and the Humboldt-Redwood Marathon. He was a member of the Dolphin Club and successfully swam the Golden Gate five times. He was a member of the Olympic Club wrestling team in San Francisco and during the winter he competed in snowmobile race events in the Tahoe area.

Mr. Healy remained at Hanna Center until 1956, when he accepted a teaching post at El Verano, and later Prestwood, elementary schools, both in Sonoma Valley. In 1961 he accepted a post at Tamalpais High School in Marin as chairman of the athletic department and was coach of the wrestling and swim teams. From 1967 to 1968 he was with the Santa Rosa Junior College physical education department, then moved to Armijo High School in Fairfield, where he served as teacher and coach.

Mr. Healy was a member of the Napa County Sheriff's Underwater Posse, and leader of that group's scuba diving team. In 1980, while taking the lead searching for the body of a policeman who had drowned the previous day in Napa's Lake Berryessa, Mr. Healy lost his life in a diving accident.

For almost 20 years, the Alumni Association of Hanna Center has remembered and paid tribute to Mr. Healy by conducting the annual Field Day events in his name.

Mr. Healy built the structure of the physical education, sports and recreation program at Hanna that has served as the foundation for this department for nearly 50 years. A role model as an athlete, husband and a gentleman, Mr. Healy serves as a continuous reminder to staff, boys and alumni of the importance of seeking excellence and of living life to its fullest.

Top: The first Field Day, August 12, 1950.

Below: Jim Healy, athletic director.

Opposite: Cover of Referee magazine, January 19, 1952. Typical benefit event for Hanna Center.

REFEREE

25c

MAGAZINE

VOL. 48 — NO. 2 63 JANUARY 19, 1952

Chavez Battles For Hanna Boys Center

Eddie Chavez shown with Father O'Connor in front of the Chapel, looking over the grounds at Hanna Boys Center in Sonoma, California. This beautiful place which includes a gymnasium, three cottages, cooking kitchen, swimming pool, recreation grounds, grazing land, etc., covers an area of 157 acres on which they raise their own vegetables, chickens, cattle, sheep, etc. The Hanna Boys Center is nonsectarian.

Chavez meets Paddy DeMarco in a ten-round rematch at San Francisco's Winterland this Thursday night, January 17th. Fifty per cent of the profits from this show will go to the Hanna Boys Center in Sonoma.

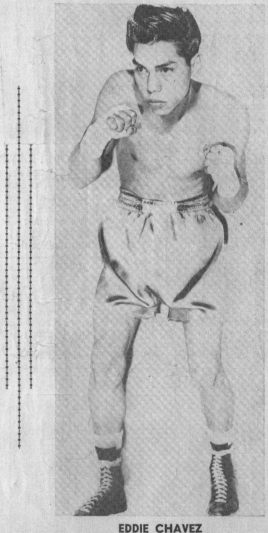

EDDIE CHAVEZ

John Brown, alumnus

"I knew the staff at the Center cared about the boys there. You can't avoid knowing that if you really want to be honest with yourself. Their caring made the difference for me." So spoke John Brown as he described the turning point of his life at Hanna Boys Center while a student from 1956 through 1960.

John came from a broken home and was placed with a foster family, but he really wasn't ready for them. He got into trouble by lying and stealing. He enrolled at Hanna Center when he was 14 years old.

"When I first went there I didn't care for it much. I really didn't care about anything, because I felt nobody cared about me," John recalled. After running away from the Center at one point, John was confronted by Father O'Connor, who told him he had to make a commitment to stay at Hanna or make his own way in the world. John realized where he was supposed to be and that Hanna was the best option for him.

John received his share of work consequences while at Hanna. Thirty years later he still recalls digging ditches, burying pipe and peeling potatoes. It was hard work, but worth it to him because of the positive changes he made while at Hanna.

John completed the Hanna program and joined the Navy, where he learned the basics of elevator repair and maintenance. It was this knowledge which led him to his career in the elevator service business, a job at which he worked for over 30 years.

When John was 14, he promised himself that someday he would have a family and that he would be a real father to his children. He fulfilled that promise when he married his wife, Gail. They were to have three children—two sons and a daughter. John found family life rewarding. One of the activities he enjoyed most was coaching Joe DiMaggio baseball teams, on which his sons played.

Another endeavor John enjoyed was helping establish the Hanna alumni association. He once told Father O'Connor that if he got 10 good men to start the association, he would make it work. With the help of his Hanna roommate, Norbert Anzano, and Frank Youngblood, another alumnus who would become John's life-long friend, John got the association established. He went on to become its first president and has served the group faithfully for more than 25 years. "We have made it successful," said John. "I did it to say 'thank you' for what I received from the Center and to let the boys know that they are not alone."

"When I look at it now, I realize that I had it better than most," said John during a recent interview. "I had a tutored education and I had people who cared and did what they had to do to get me in shape as a person. I often wonder what I might have been if I didn't go to Hanna Center. The Center does good work. It kind of grows on you."

A loving husband and father, a competent tradesman, twice president of the Hanna alumni association, John Brown is a man who has given much to his family and to his community. John has not forgotten the people who helped him during his early years—making frequent trips to the Sisters of St. Francis in Milwaukee to visit his former teachers. John turned his life around at Hanna Center, and the values he learned there and took with him have served him well through the years.

Left: John Brown (left) with his wife, Gail, and fellow alumnus, Myron MacNeil.

Above: John as a student, circa 1960.

Dedication

The Archbishop Hanna Center for Boys, as the Center was formally named, was dedicated May 21, 1950, in an impressive program conducted on the new campus. More than 7,000 persons attended the formal ceremonies under a blazing sun.

The principal speakers on that day were Archbishop John J. Mitty; California Governor Earl Warren; Hilliard Comstock, judge of the Superior Court of Sonoma County; and Daniel Flanagan, chairman of

Chairman of the Board Daniel J. Flanagan gives his dedicatory address. Note that the drape had not yet been removed from the Our Lady of Fatima statue.

ORIE DAMEWOOD

Formal Dedication

Archbishop Hanna Center for Boys

SONOMA VALLEY - MAY 21, 1950

Most Reverend John J. Mitty, Archbishop of San Francisco, Presiding

❧

Program

1. Blessing of Buildings—Most Reverend John J. Mitty, D. D.
2. Blessing of Flags — Most Reverend John J. Mitty, D. D.
3. Dedicatory Addresses:

DANIEL V. FLANAGAN
Chairman, Board of Directors

THE HONORABLE HILLIARD COMSTOCK
Judge of the Superior Court, Sonoma County

THE HONORABLE EARL WARREN
Governor of California

THE MOST REVEREND JOHN J. MITTY, D. D.
Archbishop of San Francisco

❧

Reverend John T. Foudy, Ph. D.   James Corcoran
Narrator   Carrilloneur

❧

Carillonic bells loaned by Schulmerich Electronics Inc., Sellersville, Pa.; arranged by
C. H. Kettenhofen, District Representative.
Public Address System through courtesy of James F. Waters Company.
This program through courtesy of the Santa Rosa Branch, Bank of America, N. T. & S. A.
◆ 2

the Hanna board of directors.

Archbishop Mitty began the ceremony by blessing the school building. Following the Pledge of Allegiance and the singing of the national anthem, flags presented to the Center by the Sonoma County chapters of the Veterans of Foreign Wars and the Native Sons of the Golden West were raised on the Center's flagpole. Board chairman Flanagan introduced Judge Comstock, who extended the Center and the boys a welcome from the people of the "Valley of the Moon" as the Sonoma Valley is known even today.

Governor Warren addressed the crowd, praising Hanna Boys Center as an important contribution to the youth welfare facilities of the state. "The Center is a magnificent step forward in the positive approach to giving unfortunate youngsters an equal opportunity to be prepared to meet the exigencies of life," the governor said.

In his address, Archbishop Mitty spoke of the dedication and generosity of the Center's founders and supporters. "In all my days as priest and bishop, I have never experienced anything like the development and realization of the Archbishop Hanna Center for Boys," he said. "These buildings are here because of your work and your generosity."

After the his address, His Excellency Archbishop Mitty and 15-year-old Manuel Braga, resident at the Center, unveiled a 12-foot relief statue above the entrance to the chapel. San Francisco artist Ruth Cravath sculpted the statue of Our Lady of Fatima, under whose patronage the Center had been placed.

Top left: Archbishop John J. Mitty.

Right: California Governor Earl Warren.

Left: Copy of the Formal Dedication ceremony program.

Expansion of the School and Curriculum

On September 5, 1950, the school opened for the first full year. A 10th grade curriculum was added, and with that the need for more teachers. Sister Mary Peter joined the faculty, beginning her 30-year career at Hanna Boys Center.

As enrollment continued to grow, three more classrooms were added to the school facility. By 1955, the number of teaching sisters had grown from the initial five to 10. In that year, Mother Bartholomew returned to Hanna Boys Center — not as a visitor to see how things were going, but rather as the superior of the convent and a part-time teacher in the high school division. After 12 years as mother general and six years as president of Cardinal Stritch College, at age 73, she was still a dynamic force and an inspiration to the sisters of the Franciscan community.

That same year, Sisters Ellen and Allan Marie arrived, ready to assist boys who needed more individualized instruction in the reading program. Many of the boys who came to Hanna were lacking in this skill development. In order to help them learn to read at a level of proficiency that matched their chronological years, the sisters developed an intensive literacy program. In 1967, after a new library was built on the Hanna campus, Sister Edwardine, a skilled teacher, arrived and established a reading clinic in a classroom attached to the library,

ORIE DAMEWOOD

Top: Sister Dorothy Roche in the classroom.

Bottom: Sister Clare and Sister Yvonne Therese with Father Schmitt at a Boys Town workshop, August, 1956.

Sergeant Jack Young, *friend of Hanna Center*

Each year at graduation Hanna Boys Center presents a wristwatch to the boy who demonstrates a desire to go beyond the normal requirements of the Hanna program and who upholds the highest standards in all program areas. This award is known as "The Boy of the Year." The wristwatch is donated by the family of Sergeant Jack Young in memory of the man who was Hanna Center's friend and benefactor.

A native of San Francisco, Jack Young grew up in the Sunnyside section and attended Sunnyside Grammar School, Aptos Junior High and Balboa High School. He served four years in naval intelligence during World War II. After the service he decided to enter the San Francisco Police Department, where his concern for others was almost legendary.

He married his high school sweetheart, Geraldine, and although they had no children of their own they developed an enduring family of friends from a variety of activities. They poured great energy into Hanna Boys Center. "He was a counselor and friend to these boys," said John Reilly, the Center's first caseworker.

Jack was in charge of a group named for Our Lady of Fatima. Every year, on the first Saturday of May, he and the other members would bring 40 Hanna boys to "The City" to tour the Hall of Justice and to learn that policemen were "human." The boys would go to sing at the annual policemen's Mass and later would have an outing at Playland, a popular amusement park. Jack would also visit Hanna Center once or twice each month and talk with the boys. Occasionally, he would bring them home for dinner on a weekend and then drive them back. Monsignor O'Connor said that Jack "worked with our boys all the time for 20 years helping many of them find jobs, helping them get out of trouble—and stay out."

Tragically, Sergeant Jack Young was killed by a gang of intruders at Ingleside Station in 1971 at the age of 51. At least 1,200 uniformed police and hundreds of sympathizers attended his funeral. Among those present were Father Pulskamp, Father Regan and Father O'Connor, as well as several alumni and boys of Hanna Center. Mrs. Young decided to bury her husband in Sonoma because he was so close to the boys and staff of Hanna.

His fellow police officers honor Jack Young with a plaque that hangs in the Ingleside Police Station. The inscription on the plaque reads:

"Let all who pass within these walls
Know he worked here and died here.
Know he never had a bad word about anyone.
Know he was a living example of what a man
    should be.
John was killed in Ingleside Station 29
    August 1971."

It is fitting that Hanna Boys Center honors its good friend, Jack Young, by naming "The Boy of the Year" award in his name.

Sergeant John V. Young, SFPD (with ball), at Playland-At-The-Beach, San Francisco, 1957. Left to right: child care worker Timothy Thorsen, George Ventura, Mike Tyrell and Bob Wilson.

where she worked with small groups of boys who needed additional attention and help developing their reading skills.

It was also in 1955 that Sister Yvonne Therese arrived to teach the younger boys in grade five. Mother Bartholomew encouraged her to start a Hanna Center choir. Even though this young sister claimed she had no training to attempt such an endeavor, Mother Bartholomew thought that the fact she had a good voice should be enough to begin. "You can do anything you set your mind to" was a saying often heard from "Mother B," as she was affectionately called.

And set her mind to it Sister Yvonne Therese did. Within a year, the boys were singing in four voices. She discovered beautiful soprano and alto voices in boys in the lower grades; from the upper grades came the tenors and basses. Within a few years, the Center received many requests from civic and private groups, asking for the Hanna Boys Choir to come and sing. They were trained in Gregorian chant and polyphonic music, and they had a repertoire that included many folk songs and a long list of Christmas carols that went as far back as the 16th century.

Skills that the sisters didn't know they had often came to the fore. Sister Mary Peter had started "Hanna Haps," the school newspaper, originally produced on an old mimeograph machine. Sister Carmel Therese influenced boys in the areas of speech and drama. Sister Allan Marie made costumes for plays; all her creations came from found items, ranging from old drapery material to the pampas grass that grew along the creek bed.

Top: Sister Yvonne Therese with the choir at KGO-TV studio, San Francisco.

Bottom: Sister Ferdinanda working in the kitchen.

Roy Willmarth, *woodshop teacher*

In the 39 years Roy Willmarth served at Hanna Boys Center, he was an inspiration to his students and fellow faculty colleagues. As instructor and head of the manual training department, he combined no-nonsense discipline with a sense of humor and dedication to helping the boys he taught.

"I will always remember Mr. Willmarth as being very giving to myself and other boys here," said Joshua Peters, a 1992 Hanna resident.

Mr. Willmarth was born in 1928 in Wisconsin and graduated from Stout University there. In 1953 he was hired by Father William O'Connor to head the shop department for Hanna Center—a position he retained until his death in 1992.

When Mr. Willmarth arrived at the Hanna campus, the shop classroom was not yet completed—and so initially he had to improvise, even using part of the dining room at the Center for instruction until essential equipment arrived.

During his tenure at the Center, Mr. Willmarth was known for his sense of humor—and his sense of discipline. "Sure, he might be a little on the tough side, but his being tough on us taught us to respect each staff member no matter how tough or easy we thought them to be," remembered Hanna student Carl Kitley.

Students and faculty members alike remember that Mr. Willmarth also brought complete dedication to his job.

"Roy had been at Hanna Boys Center almost as long as there has been a Hanna Center," said faculty member Dolores Jaehrling. "It was an integral part of his life."

Even after being diagnosed with cancer in 1991, Mr. Willmarth continued to teach at Hanna. "Even when he was very sick he used to come here and, as he put it, 'be here just so the wood shop could be open,' " remembered Peters.

Mr. Willmarth was also committed to the larger community during the years he lived in Sonoma, serving as secretary for the Sonoma Kiwanis Club. He and his wife, Rose, later moved to Napa, where she and their son, Michael, currently live. Their son, Mark, lives in Southern California.

Mr. Willmarth died March 3, 1992, during a visit to his mother in Wisconsin. A memorial service was held at Hanna Boys Center, at which teachers and students shared their fond memories of him.

Top: Roy Willmarth.

Bottom: Roy Willmarth with a boy at the drillpress.

The sisters were also responsible for supervision of the dining hall and the Center's daily meals. Although the chapel was always considered the heart of the campus, the kitchen ranked a very close second. Here the boys not only received their three square meals a day; they were also trained in various jobs as waiters, bus boys, dish washers and cooks' assistants. The sisters in charge of the kitchen worked long hours, planning and preparing meals as well as supervising the boys who were hired and assigned to the various jobs. Under the watchful eye of Sister Augusta, and then later Sister Anna Marie, the boys performed their duties with high standards. At Christmas, hundreds of cookies were baked and decorated, then placed in boxes or tins to be delivered to staff and benefactors.

By 1960, the number of sisters assigned to Hanna Boys Center reached 12. There were now more nuns residing at the Center than ever before during a school year, and the number would remain steady for three years. Sisters Mary Grace, Mary Clare, Mary Peter, Elizabeth and Mona were familiar names almost since the beginning of Hanna Boys Center; they were now joined by other sisters, some of whom were later called back to Milwaukee for other duties, to be replaced by Sisters Virgine, Philomene and Alberta.

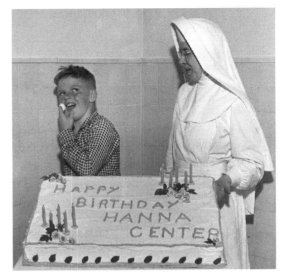

Above: Sister Augusta gets help testing frosting for Hanna's fifth birthday.

Below: Airmen from Travis Air Force Base bring baseball equipment for the boys, December, 1957. Pictured with Sister Grace and Sister Peter.

The Choir

Through the years 1956 through 1964, Hanna had an outstanding boys' choir performing under the direction of Sister Yvonne Therese.

The choir received performance requests from a variety of Bay Area groups and institutions. Among these were the California Producers' Association at the Fairmont Hotel, the Sonoma Woman's Club, the Sonoma Community Center, St. Joseph's Hospital in San Francisco and Memorial Hospital in Santa Rosa, Oakland Serra Club, Rosenberg's Department Store and the Christmas party and program at Hanna Center.

In 1959, the choir performed in Union Square in San Francisco as part of the kickoff of the annual spring fund-raising drive of The Guardsmen, a San Francisco charitable organization.

On December 5, 1963, Coast Recording Company in San Francisco was the scene of a four-hour recording session. The choir cut a 12-inch record consisting of holiday and liturgical music.

The Christmas season brought many requests for the performance of the choir. One year the choir's appearances included taping two television programs. KGO-TV, Channel 7, featured various school choirs from the Bay Area in a Christmas broadcast and included the Hanna choir in the program; KRON-TV, Channel 4, presented the choir on the "Catholic Heritage" program, with Val King as host.

The choir was also heard on radio broadcasts throughout the Bay Area. Radio station KSRO presented the choir in a special program on Christmas Day in 1963.

It was an honor to be in the Hanna Center Choir. Besides a sense of worth and accomplishment in this skill, each boy looked forward to May when, encouraged by Sgt. Jack Young, a group of San Francisco Police officers invited the boys to sing at a special Mass at Saint Joseph's. This was followed by breakfast at a well-known restaurant and a day at Playland, a very popular amusement park in San Francisco.

The choir contained as many as 36 voices—a high percentage of the residents of Hanna Center at that time. Asked what problems she encountered in organizing the boys' choir, Sister Yvonne Therese replied, "First of all, our boys are in the 11 to 17-year-old bracket, and so we have voice changes. A soprano voice this month may suddenly become an alto in March. So we must keep recruiting sopranos, for example. Or if we have an overabundance of altos we go to work on new music to take advantage of the voice mix."

COURTESY OF SAN FRANCISCO PROGRESS

Over the years the choir developed an amazingly high-quality sound and could perform songs in foreign languages, especially Latin and German. The choir was an excellent resource for the boys and provided many opportunities for the public to learn more about the work being done at Hanna Center.

Sing it to the Marines! The Hanna Boys Center choir are joined in their rendition of The Marines' Hymn by Major General James P. Berkeley, commanding general of the Marine Corps' Department of the Pacific. The singing in Union Square was part of the kickoff of the annual spring fundraising drive of The Guardsmen, a San Francisco charitable organization, May, 1959.

New Facilities

During this period of expansion and increasing enrollment, the necessity of enlarging the campus facilities became clear. The first priority was to increase the dormitory space for boys' living quarters, and plans were drawn up for three additional cottages.

Hanna's need for the additional living quarters was made known to industry, labor and business leaders in 1953. Charles L. Harney, San Francisco engineering contractor and chairman of the Center's board of directors, led the effort, marshalling resources and seeking donations of labor and materials. Groundbreaking for the new construction was conducted at a ceremony on June 25, 1953.

Labor, management and materials valued at $250,000 were donated by industry members throughout the state. Volunteer labor-management teams, numbering as many as 150 men in a single day, worked weekends for six months to complete the cottages.

One day the framing for two of the houses rose from the ground in less than 10 hours—the result of a unique contest. Two 75-man teams of the Carpenter's Union, Local 22, raced each other to build the cottages. They not only donated their labor, but also gave the Center an additional check for $1,000. Other union craftsmen who donated their

Groundbreaking ceremony for three new cottages, June 25, 1953. Identified in the picture, left to right: Sister Clare, Charles L. Harney (chairman of the Board of Directors), Monsignor Flanagan, Father O'Connor, boys and guests.

labor included 25 plumbers led by Mike Desiano, a San Francisco plumbing and heating contractor; workers from the Roofers' Union, Local 40; and 15 sheet metal workers guided by Robert Tuck, president of Atlas Heating and Ventilating Company.

The three cottages—named Saint Joseph's, Notre Dame and Mount Alverno—were dedicated June 20, 1954. "Appreciation Day" ceremonies were held to honor the members of the construction industry and unions who had contributed so generously to the project. Some 750 ceremony attendees were thanked for their efforts, and Hanna boys presented a plaque and scroll to Charles Harney. Union carpenter Russell Hintz, a former Hanna boy, gave a brief speech in which he expressed his gratitude for being able to repay the Center in some measure by contributing his time and labor to the project.

Further additions to the campus were started in June of 1955, with work beginning on three classrooms and a trade school. A dental clinic was donated by Dr. E. E. Keeffe in July of 1956. The Kearney Auditorium, constructed with donations from Mary Kearney in memory of her husband, Patrick Kearney, along with additions to the trade school and to the administration building, were completed February 1, 1957.

Through a generous gift of the Raskob Foundation for Catholic Activities, the John J. Raskob Memorial Infirmary building was constructed and dedicated on May 10, 1960. Sister Cordelia arrived that summer as the Center's first full-time nurse. Each morning before school started, she would give treatment to any boy who did not feel well or who was there for some

BARNEY PETERSON

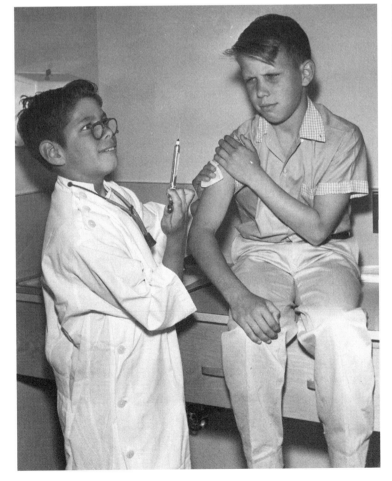

Opposite top: A boy tries his hand at the tractor with help from engineer William Harmon.

Opposite bottom: The construction crew with Father O'Connor.

Above: "Carpenters' Day," November 21, 1953.

Left: Promotion photo for the dedication of the new infirmary, May 10, 1960.

Below: You couldn't fool Father Regan.

prescribed medication; the same procedure took place after school. Sister Cordelia was literally on call 24 hours a day. There were times, such as flu season, when the four-bed ward was filled, as well as all of the private rooms.

A stained glass window was installed in the chapel in May of 1962, and a marble floor in December of that year. Alternate water systems for the Center were incorporated in June of 1963, while a storage building was completed in August. For the school, a new arts and crafts room and an audio visual room were added in March of 1964. A backstop for the baseball field was erected in February of 1964, with a bronze plaque reading, "Gift of Phi Beta Kappa Delta Judge Quayle."

The capacity of the Center increased to 120 boys, and on January 28, 1965, the 1,000th boy, Theodore Dominguez, was enrolled in the program.

Above: From left, San Francisco contractor Ed Larkin, Father O'Connor, 13-year-old Johnny Green and Joe O'Sullivan, business agent for Carpenters Union Local 22.

Below: The construction crew poses with Monsignor Flanagan by the chapel.

The Stained Glass Window

"Come to Me, you who are troubled..."

To know the heart of Hanna Boys Center is to know the story of the magnificent stained glass window in the Chapel.

One day in 1958, eight years after the Center had opened, a woman visited. Monsignor O'Connor showed her around, ending up in the chapel.

The woman said, "I'd love to do something for the Center." Monsignor O'Connor looked at the side wall of the Chapel, with its large amber-colored windows, and stated simply, "A stained glass window would be beautiful in this chapel."

The woman made no comment and left. Some time later, Monsignor O'Connor received notice from Chartres, France, that a window had been commissioned for the Center chapel. Monsignor O'Connor sent the dimensions for the window, along with a theme: the words of Jesus, "Come to Me, all you who are troubled..." with an image of the Lord surrounded by 12 boys from all ethnic backgrounds.

Three years later, in 1961, word came from Chartres that the window was on its way to Sonoma. It arrived in 32 panes, each weighing 200 pounds, with the entire window covering an area of 512 square feet.

The figure of Jesus and those 12 boys has bathed the chapel in soft blues and reds since the day it was installed and has looked down on hundreds of boys as they have knelt in the chapel, offering their daily morning prayers and their worship on Sundays.

The real beauty of the window is that to this day, no one at the Center knows who donated it. Monsignor O'Connor was convinced that it was the woman who stopped by one afternoon in 1958, but he was not absolutely certain. The window serves as a constant reminder that everything at the

Center is a gift and that ultimately it is the power of God that untangles the confusion, enlightens the doubts, and heals the wounds of Hanna's boys and families.

The window, created by artist Gabriel Loire of Chartres, France, was installed by Alois Moser of Santa Monica on May 24, 1962. Dedication took place as part of Hanna's 13th birthday "open house" attended by several hundred visitors on November 25, 1962. Monsignor O'Connor, assisted by Father Gerald Cox, blessed the window during a special service in the chapel.

Above: Detail of the stained glass window.

A Day in the Life of a Sister of St. Francis

A day in the life of a sister at Hanna began at 5:30 a.m. The early morning hours were spent together at Mass, meditation and chanting the Office of The Blessed Virgin Mary.

After breakfast, and before going to the classroom, various tasks were performed. Some sisters went up to clean the priests' house, another went to the chapel to do the work of sacristan. Others went into the kitchen to supervise boys who were working there or in the dining room areas. Another would go to the infirmary with Sister Cordelia to assist in receiving boys who needed treatment. There were no janitors assigned to the areas in which the sisters worked. Each sister had the responsibility to clean and maintain her own classroom. With the help of the boys who wished to earn extra money or needed to work off hours given for disciplinary means, the sisters saw to it that floors were waxed and polished in the classrooms, the chapel, the kitchen and the infirmary.

From left to right, Sisters Romuald, Edwardine, Clare and Aloysine.

The boys liked being with the sisters, and the sisters worked right along with them. On Saturday mornings the convent, the priests' house, the boys' dining rooms and the kitchen were cleaned thoroughly. Most Saturday afternoons the teaching sisters worked in their classrooms, preparing lessons and planning bulletin boards. They were well aware that thorough preparation geared to meeting the needs of each boy greatly assisted in deterring discipline problems.

Though prayer and work were primary in a sister's life, recreation was certainly deemed important. Relaxation was built into the schedule after the dinner hour in the evening. Card games, visiting with one another, reading, and watching TV were activities the sisters enjoyed. For many years, many of the sisters appreciated swimming in a private pool offered by a family who lived near downtown Sonoma. In her mid-70s, Mother Bartholomew learned how to swim.

During the six-week period of summer school, several Sisters of St. Francis who worked during the school year at St. Robert's Parish in San Bruno came to teach at Hanna, sometimes accompanied by sisters from Milwaukee. Their arrival afforded the Hanna Center sisters the time to take courses at various colleges or universities or return to the motherhouse in Milwaukee for other assignments.

Ann Healy, *executive secretary*

To work for one organization for over 50 years is a remarkable achievement. To dedicate an entire life to the service of youth and to serve an organization with love, dedication and skill for that many years creates an incomparable legacy. Mrs. Ann Healy has achieved both of these feats during her outstanding career at Hanna Boys Center.

Born in Omaha, Nebraska, Ann Healy was the youngest child in a family of five girls and two boys. She attended South High School in Omaha before starting work with Boys Town in September of 1941 (at age 18) in its downtown Omaha mailroom, for $12 a week.

She soon discovered that she did not like the tedious task of mailroom duty. When her supervisor noted in her resume that she was a trained stenographer, she asked Ann if she would like to be transferred to work at Boys Town, doing stenographic work. She said yes.

This was about the time of the Japanese attack on Pearl Harbor, which officially brought the U.S. into World War II. Ann's mother wanted her to go to work in some kind of plant involved in the war effort, noting that the pay was much higher. But when Boys Town offered her $25 a week, her mother said it was all right to stay.

Ann started work at the Boys Town campus on December 8, 1941 (the day after the attack on Pearl Harbor), and eventually took dictation from the famed Father Flanagan, founding director.

Her husband-to-be, Jim Healy, was already at Boys Town in the athletic department. Ann and Jim met in 1948, before Jim left to work at Hanna Boys Center. He returned to Omaha on a visit in 1949, and he and Ann were married in the chapel on the Boys Town campus. On their honeymoon, the newlyweds traveled to Sonoma, California, where Mrs. Healy was promptly recruited by Father William O'Connor, director of Hanna Center, as his secretary.

Monsignor James Pulskamp, who succeeded Monsignor O'Connor as director of Hanna Center, recalled his mentor often describing Mrs. Healy as "the world's best secretary."

Pulskamp, presently Chancellor of the Santa Rosa Diocese and for the past six years pastor of Holy Spirit Church, offered the following comments about Mrs. Healy during a recent interview:

"Ann could run the place. She is very competent, can anticipate and reads people well.

Mrs. Ann Healy

She always seemed to be a step ahead of you. She got to know many of the donors (to the Center) and kept in contact with them. She had a sense of public relations and regularly dropped personal notes to friends of Hanna. Moreover, she made it a point to become acquainted with the boys and followed their progress."

Often when former boys return as men to the Center for a visit they will stop by to see Mrs. Healy. She greets them with a hug and says, "I remember you, you served Mass for Father O'Connor," or "you were very close to Mr. John Reilly," as she remembers something personal about each one. Soon the former boy and Mrs. Healy will have tears in their eyes as they reminisce about earlier events and years gone by. Her caring and personal touch is the embodiment of what Hanna Boys Center is all about.

Mrs. Healy's love of Hanna Center has been manifested by her steadfast recording of the major events and historical facts about the Center. Without her devotion to keeping files on every important event involving the Center—from 1949 to the present—much of its history, including many of the wonderful pictures presented in this book, would not have been recorded.

Mrs. Healy was at Hanna at the beginning and has been an integral part of the success and growth of the Center. She continues to serve the boys and staff of Hanna with the same standard of excellence and sense of purpose that she brought with her from Boys Town in 1949.

A New Director

By 1972, Hanna Boys Center was firmly established and was recognized as one of the finest residential treatment centers in the country. A great deal had been accomplished since 1946 under Father O'Connor's leadership—the successful pilot program, the campaign for funds, the plans for construction and site selection, the opening of the Center, arrival of boys, program development, day-to-day operation, and expansion of the campus facilities—a lifetime of work for any man.

There had been many pressures over the years on the director, now a monsignor. There was a constant financial balancing act to perform, and fund-raising was a persistent need. Shortages of trained staff, particularly child care workers, required consistent recruiting and training efforts. The desire to enroll more boys and reduce the waiting list weighed heavily on Monsignor O'Connor's mind. He had reached his 65th birthday and decided it was time to allow a younger man to assume leadership of the Center.

Representing 125 years of service at Hanna Boys Center on December 4, 1975.

From left: Monsignor O'Connor, John Guillaumin, Sister Clare, Sister Grace and Ann Healy.

On October 1, 1972, Monsignor William L. O'Connor resigned as director of Hanna Boys Center. On the occasion of his resignation he issued the following statement:

"During the past year, I have participated in making decisions which will enlarge the Center's role in caring for needy Western boys. With an expanded program in the offing, I recently withdrew from my post as director of the Center in the belief that this is an especially appropriate time for vigorous young leadership. Having spent more than a quarter of a century in the founding and development of Hanna Center, I would not wish to leave, and will remain here as associate director."

The Most Reverend Mark Hurley, bishop of Santa Rosa, accepted the resignation reluctantly, stating, "Not only has Monsignor O'Connor accomplished the multitude of tasks assigned to him with efficiency, but he did so with exceptional kindness, good humor, sympathetic understanding and personal friendliness."

The bishop further complimented the director with these words: "His complete naturalness, his sincerity and his genuine humility has charmed the most distressed child as well as the most successful adult among those with whom he has come into contact."

Monsignor O'Connor had served as director of the Center for 23 years, since its opening in December of 1949. His successor, the Reverend Father James Pulskamp, paid tribute to his mentor, saying, "Monsignor O'Connor's recent decision to retire from directorship of Hanna Center brought a sense of loss to all of us here, but a loss softened by the fact that he will remain an important figure in the administration of our program for youngsters."

Father Pulskamp had served as associate director of the Center since July 1, 1970. He had worked closely with Monsignor O'Connor during those years, in addition to the three summers that he served at Hanna while a seminarian training for the priesthood. Father Pulskamp was Monsignor O'Connor's first choice to assume the reins of the Center. Thus began a new era in the history of Hanna Boys Center, under the leadership of Father James Pulskamp.

ORIE DAMEWOOD

Monsignor O'Connor, shortly before stepping down as director, chats with a Hanna boy.

Father James Pulskamp with boys.

CHAPTER 3

The Pulskamp Years 1972–1984

Keeping the Dream Alive

Chances are that if a former resident returned to Hanna Boys Center for a visit in 1975, he would say, "Things sure have changed around here—it was a lot harder and a lot stricter when I was here in 1955." Chances are that if a former resident returned in 1995, he would say the same thing about life at Hanna in 1975. Each succession of boys wants to believe that they were "pioneers" in some fashion.

However, the reality remains that the program Father Pulskamp implemented was virtually the same one Father O'Connor and his staff developed when the Center first opened. The goals, objectives, standards and values of the Center remained constant through the O'Connor years, and Father Pulskamp would guard those values and

Father Pulskamp visits with boys in a Hanna cottage at Christmas time.

standards and improve upon the Center's ability to meet those goals whenever he could.

Father Pulskamp's style of management was marked by his direct involvement in many aspects of the program. He conducted formal weekly meetings with the school principal, caseworkers, and other department heads. During his years as director he had the opportunity to hire two school principals, Chester Sharek and Bob McInnis. Simultaneously, he found time to interact with the boys and would visit with them often, especially in the evenings.

Despite the changes Father Pulskamp initiated, the basic program Hanna Center offered boys and their families remained largely unaltered. When a boy was accepted for placement at the Center, immediate pressure in a very tense family situation was often alleviated. The overall program addressed problem areas each boy faced: school, group living and family upheaval.

The precepts on which the Hanna program was based were as effective when Father Pulskamp ended his term as director in 1984 as when Father O'Connor inaugurated the Hanna program in 1949. At some level, the boys who graduated from the Center understood the value of these goals and standards—even though they might still believe that they had it rougher when they were at Hanna.

Father Pulskamp with three lads.

Father James Pulskamp, director

Monsignor James E. Pulskamp has no doubt that his coming to Hanna Center was preordained.

A member of a devoted Catholic family in Marin County, as an eight year old he was among the 10,000 in attendance, along with his parents, brother and sister, at the groundbreaking ceremonies for Hanna Boys Center in Sonoma on September 19, 1948.

"Then, to become director some 23 years later? It was just meant to be," he said during a recent interview.

Monsignor Pulskamp, the second of only three priests to have served as executive director of Hanna Boys Center, defines his years at the Center as both "a unique experience" and "a gift from God."

It was while a student at St. Patrick's Seminary in Menlo Park that the young Jim Pulskamp became acquainted first-hand with Hanna Center by spending three summers assisting counselors in the cottages, learning much about the boys and program. "Father O'Connor had his eye on him even back then," recalled Mrs. Ann Healy, Hanna's veteran executive secretary.

Ordained a priest April 29, 1967, Father Pulskamp served as associate pastor at St. Vincent de Paul Church, Petaluma, for a year before taking graduate courses at San Francisco State College and San Diego State College. He acquired his master's degree in social work in 1970, the year he was named associate director of Hanna Boys Center at the age of 29.

When longtime executive director Monsignor O'Connor stepped down, Father Pulskamp was moved to the top post, and he officially assumed the role on October 1, 1972.

After announcing Father Pulskamp as his successor, Monsignor O'Connor, at his own request, was reassigned as associate director, working side-by-side with his young protégé until his retirement in 1984, the same year Father Pulskamp was appointed chancellor of the Catholic Diocese of Santa Rosa.

He and his mentor, Monsignor O'Connor, proved to be a great team. "With the difference in our ages, it was like a father-son relationship," said Monsignor Pulskamp.

Mrs. Healy recalls their ritualistic greeting each day in the administration building: "Good morning, Father William," was Pulskamp's standard greeting to his superior. "Good morning, Father James" was always O'Connor's smiling response.

The tall (6'4") young priest with the engaging smile immediately clicked with the boys at Hanna. During his 11 years as director, his homilies at Mass on Sundays were prepared with the boys in mind, and his gifted delivery and depth of feeling, coupled with his great sense of humor, reached the boys and adults in attendance.

He not only knew the name of each boy at the Center, but also his individualized program, and Father Pulskamp was involved with the progress of each boy. He regularly made evening visits to the cottages to see the boys and check with staff.

Among Pulskamp's poignant memories of those visits are when "the little ones" would rush up to hug him. "That special bonding between yourself and the kids is such a strong factor," he said, "almost a father category.

"There was a trust there. Tenderness and love, therapeutic in nature. The kids felt it. I felt it. Boys who left the Center would later write me a letter of appreciation, or call on the telephone. Like the one who said, 'I looked upon you as a father to me. I just wanted to say thanks. You stood by me.'

"I called these my child-rearing years—with staff, we helped turn their lives around, working as a team."

Monsignor Pulskamp said that Hanna Boys Center enriched other people's lives as well as his own. "Among them are the members of the board of directors who volunteer their valuable time and

talent down through the years. It has been an honor to be associated with such wonderful people."

Named reverend monsignor in May of 1985, Pulskamp currently serves as pastor of Holy Spirit parish in Santa Rosa, in addition to being chancellor of the sprawling Diocese of Santa Rosa (which

extends from the Sonoma and Napa valleys to the Oregon border).

As director emeritus of Hanna Center, Monsignor Pulskamp is also a member of the board of directors and even today continues a close association with the men and women who serve on the board.

A Day in the Life of a Hanna Boy

"Good morning," calls the child care worker, as she awakens the boys with a cheery greeting and the hard reality of an overhead light. The typical Hanna day starts early—6:30 a.m.—during the school year. The boys need to get moving—there's a lot to accomplish.

After a quick face wash, brushing of teeth, and combing of hair, the boys have a few minutes to make their beds and straighten out their bedrooms. They quickly learn to work with their roommate in readying their room for the coming inspection check by the staff. When all is judged to be adequate, they are off to complete their cottage chores.

It takes a joint effort to keep a cottage neat, clean and orderly when 12 youngsters are living together under one roof. The jobs are well defined and are divided evenly for efficiency. When the chores are done and have passed inspection, it is time to put away the tools and cleaning materials, and then to grab backpacks, books, and jackets and proceed as a group to the chapel.

NED DAVIS

Morning prayer in the chapel has been a tradition at Hanna since 1949. The prayer to St. Francis of Assisi has been a consistent favorite among the boys ("Lord make me an instrument of Your peace..."). The boys also ask God's blessing on all former residents and benefactors of the Center.

At last, it's chow time. Breakfast in the dining hall is served family style with the boys eating together in their cottage groups. Boys take turns serving as waiters, and some have paid jobs as dish washers, pots and pans scrubbers, and staff waiters. Of course, there is grace offered before the meal and a thanksgiving prayer after the meal.

Making the bed is job #1.

Opposite, top: Learning keyboarding techniques.

Bottom: Caring for the animals.

There are only 25 minutes for breakfast, because class begins at 8:10 a.m. Each class lasts 50 minutes, and the boys have to pay attention and take care of business, because they receive a citizenship score for their behavior in each class. A trip to the gymnasium for some physical education and exercise is sure to be part of every school day. With math, history, woodshop, art, music, English and religion it's easy to understand why the boys get hungry so soon. Lunch is 12:10 through

12:40 p.m. Then it's back to the classes for more instruction (spelling, gardening, reading, computer science, animal husbandry) until 2:10 p.m.

When the final school bell rings, it's a rush to the cottage for a quick snack. Peanut butter and jelly and a glass of milk go a long way in fortifying a boy for the group process meeting. "Group" (as it's called) can be many things—fun, difficult, boring, exciting, educational or enlightening—but it's always 45 minutes long. Problems are solved, plans are made, work is divided, differences are settled, feelings are expressed and compromises are made. "Group" can often be like medicine; the boys may not like it, but they need it.

NED DAVIS

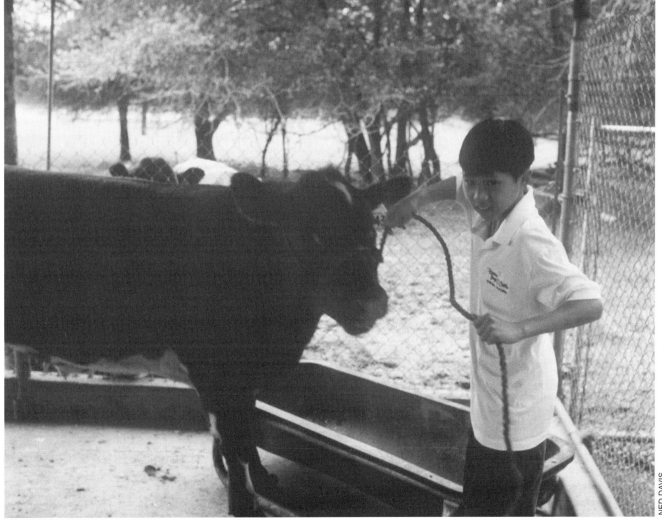

NED DAVIS

Thomas Chin, *alumnus*

As one of the first Hanna boys to make the transition into adulthood via Hanna's group homes, Tom Chin is now one of Hanna's greatest supporters, having served on the board of directors and with the alumni association. "It's hard to turn your back when you've gotten so much help," he said. "You're successful because of your past, and you have to remember that."

Tom Chin was born in San Francisco in 1954 and came to Hanna Boys Center at the age of 12, in 1965. While at Hanna, Tom received instruction from Monsignor William O'Connor, John Reilly, Sister Cordelia, and Roy Willmarth, and recalled that his education covered more than academics. "My life has been greatly influenced by my stay at Hanna Boys Center—from the basic needs of food, shelter, and education, to athletics and spiritual growth," he said.

Tom left the Sonoma campus in 1968 and took up residence at Hanna's group home in Napa, where he lived with five other boys and attended Justin High School (now Justin-Siena). He recalled that the living arrangement gave him independence without sacrificing structure and discipline.

COURTESY OF TOM CHIN

"Instead of living at Hanna we lived in the outside world, so to speak, but we were under its supervision," he said.

After three years at Justin, Tom switched to Santa Rosa High School for his senior year and graduated in 1972. That year was the first in which Hanna Boys Center offered scholarship opportunities for former residents, and Tom obtained funding to attend St. Mary's College in Moraga, California. At college, Tom majored in business and economics, and upon graduation in 1976 embarked upon a career, working for World Savings Bank. He then went on to work as a sales representative for Mobil Chemical Corporation and as a marketing manager for Woodland Poly, a manufacturer of polyethylene products. Since 1996 he has worked in sales at Vanguard Packaging in San Leandro, California. In 1986 Tom obtained his MBA at Golden Gate University.

Tom married his wife Gail in 1981—"the same year as Charles and Diana," he recalled—and they have three children: Jenna, 13; Alex, 12; and Bradley, 6. The lessons Tom learned at Hanna serve him well in his family life, he said.

"I have a beautiful family—a wife and three children—whom I can provide with the same love and understanding that I learned from being with dedicated people (at Hanna)," he said.

In addition to his roles in the workplace and as a father, Tom returned to Hanna, serving on the board of directors since 1986; he has been an active member of the alumni association, serving as secretary/treasurer, and said he enjoys introducing people to Hanna Boys Center and its mission. "It's really nice to talk to people who've not heard of it, and let them know," he said. "Hanna Boys Center is still a big part of my life."

Above: Mr. and Mrs. Tom Chin and children.

Left: Tom Chin (center) at his induction to the Hanna Board of Directors, with Bishop Steinbock (left) and Father Crews.

After "group" it's activity time. Boys on sports teams report to the gym, court, field, mat, or pool for practice. Others might work on crafts in the cottage. Some may choose to lounge and listen to music in their room. For the misbehaving it's time to atone for misdeeds by performing discipline work—the dreaded "hours." Hours may take the form of weeding, raking, washing windows, mopping floors or other cleaning chores. Or, discipline might involve writing assignments, writing apologies or otherwise undoing the wrong that has been done. Discipline at Hanna is always administered to teach, never to punish. The boys soon learn that discipline is good for the soul.

There is just enough time to wash hands before dinner at 6:00 p.m., when once again it's back to the dining hall. After dinner, there are 45 minutes of free time when the boys may choose to go to the recreation hall for a game of pool or table tennis or, on hot nights, for a quick swim.

Like morning prayers, evening showers have been a tradition at Hanna since its inception. It's good to be clean and fresh when a boy sits down at his desk for his supervised homework period. Homework time is quiet time as the boys complete their school assignments. Child care workers are there to assist, proofread and hear spelling words.

Top: Free time at the cottage.

Above: Hard at it during study period.

What? It's already 9:00 p.m.? Time for just one hour of television viewing or listening to favorite music.

Then it's night prayers time—a final gathering of cottage members to review the day, compliment each other, settle down, and pray for special intentions.

Ten o'clock is bedtime and lights out. Better get some rest—6:30 a.m. comes early, and that child care worker soon will be calling "good morning" once again.

John Reilly, *first caseworker*

In his 41 years as a counselor at Hanna Boys Center, John Reilly served as residential counselor and caseworker—playing such a crucial role in the growth of the Center that he received not only respect from his colleagues and the boys he supervised, but also recognition from the Pope.

Mr. Reilly was born February 16, 1915, in Fort Dodge, Iowa, the son of Bernard and Ellen Reilly, members of pioneer families. Mr. Reilly attended Corpus Christi School in Fort Dodge and graduated from Creighton Prep in Omaha, Nebraska. He then attended Creighton University before attending and graduating from the University of Minnesota. He participated in the American Scholar program at Trinity College in Dublin, Ireland, and at the Sorbonne in Paris, France. Mr. Reilly also received counseling credentials from Catholic University in Washington, D.C., and from the University of California at Berkeley.

Mr. Reilly served in World War II as an infantry officer in the Seventh Infantry Division and in the PAC Corps in the Pacific. When he returned to the United States, he worked with the American Cancer Society, and then considered a career teaching English to immigrant Mexican workers in Arizona. Instead, in 1951 Mr. Reilly came to Hanna on the advice of a friend, who'd arranged a meeting for him with center co-founder Monsignor William O'Connor. On the very day he met Father O'Connor, he was hired as the Center's first caseworker.

"I think the thing that attracted me to work with the kids, and attracted me all along, is the courage of the boys," Mr. Reilly said. "A lot of them come from backgrounds where they have no reason to trust adults. Out here it's a lot easier to trust. They seem to show their appreciation more. Really, it's pretty inspiring."

Shortly after his arrival at Hanna, Mr. Reilly began supervising 20 boys per cottage, after taking over from a colleague who fell ill; it was a challenge he relished.

"I liked it right from the first, but I didn't know the boys' names, and that was the hard part," Mr. Reilly recalled.

Mr. Reilly then helped purchase and maintain Hanna's three off-campus group homes, and counseled and supervised the residents. "The Center was small at the time and you were an essential part of the boys' lives. We developed a terrific feeling of loyalty," Mr. Reilly said.

In 1992, after 41 years at the center, Mr. Reilly decided to retire. At the Center's graduation ceremony on June 12, Monsignor James Pulskamp surprised Mr. Reilly by presenting him with the Pro Ecclesia et Pontifice Medal—an honor bestowed by the Pope, in recognition of his service to Hanna Center. Mr. Reilly knew nothing of the honor he was to receive until Monsignor Pulskamp called him from the chapel audience to accept the medal.

Mr. Reilly lived in Sonoma with his sister, Mary Bernadine Reilly, and was active in the local community as a member of the Knights of Columbus and the American Legion. He was also a member of the Association of Christian Therapists. Mr. Reilly died July 1, 1998, in Sonoma, at the age of 88.

John Reilly accepts the coveted Pro Ecclesia et Pontifice medal from Monsignor James E. Pulskamp.

Individual Counseling

One major change that Father Pulskamp implemented was an increased emphasis on individual counseling for the boys. He expanded the counseling staff of the Center and required the counselors to involve the boys' parents in the process to a greater degree than previously. The individualized plan for each boy was enriched to include a more comprehensive outline of target areas for his treatment. These target areas listed specific goals for changes in behavior. This type of plan also proved to be an effective measuring tool to assess each boy's progress.

Father Pulskamp attended each treatment planning review session, thereby keeping himself abreast of the boys' progress, enabling him to have direct input on treatment issues and, by his presence, giving greater emphasis to the importance of the treatment planning and review process. This new approach coincided with the hiring of consulting psychiatrist Natalie O'Byrne, M.D., who replaced retiring psychiatrist Carl Jonas, M.D., in March of 1972.

Sister Grace and John Reilly counseling a Hanna boy.

In 1973, Father Pulskamp enrolled the 1,500th boy in the Hanna program. It was during his directorship that the alumni association held its charter meeting in 1974, the beginning of an organization that would serve the boys and the Center well from then on.

Campus Renovations

By the Center's 25th anniversary in December of 1974, the cottages were starting to show the wear and tear that groups of rambunctious boys can inflict on their dwellings. Father Pulskamp initiated a program for the renovation of all six cottages. From January through October, 1975, Notre Dame cottage served as administrative offices as the administration building was expanded and remodeled. In February of 1976 a new barber shop was opened in the administrative building. A TV antenna and transmitter were installed in March of 1976 to bring broadcasts to the entire Center.

In July of 1983, work began on a $500,000 project that included adding a bedroom to each cottage, relocating the carports, replacing the heating systems, and grading and paving the cottage play areas. When these projects were completed in February of 1984, plans were begun to remodel and expand the kitchen and dining areas.

John Donahue, *director of finance and administration*

All who worked for and with John Donahue, the first director of finance and administration at Hanna Boys Center, who served from 1972 to 1985, were extremely impressed by his knowledge and foresight on any issue that affected the

Center. It was not only a learning experience, but also a genuine pleasure to witness his caring, concern, and commitment for the boys at Hanna Boys Center.

To all of the staff and boys, Mr. Donahue displayed a vigorous thrust for accomplishment and achievement. He could be a firm, determined strategist and tactician, but always demonstrated empathy and understanding toward the people influenced by these decisions. Not shy about putting in extra hours, Mr. Donahue could be found in his Hanna office every Saturday, where he put in a full day's work.

Mrs. Ann Healy recalled how impressed she was with Mr. Donahue's keen intelligence, particularly his grasp and understanding of legal matters. Mr. Donahue and his secretary, Gertrude

Henderson, formed an excellent team that contributed to the high professional standards of the administrative staff at Hanna.

A native of San Francisco, Mr. Donahue was a resident of Santa Rosa, California, where he was a member of Star of the Valley Catholic Church and an active member in numerous Catholic charities. He served as president of the Serra Club of San Francisco, president of St. Mary's College of California Alumni Association, board chairman of the Catholic Social Services of San Francisco, and was a former member of the Olympic Club of San Francisco, as well as being a member of many other professional business organizations. Mr. Donahue was also a veteran of the U. S. Marine Corps.

John Donahue, a kind and gifted administrator, worked unselfishly at Hanna Boys Center for 13 years. Often in intense pain during his latter years of service, he kept working in spite of it. He passed away after a long illness at age 56 on March 23, 1985. He was truly a generous and thoughtful man.

In Mr. Donahue's memory, and in appreciation of his dedication to the Center, the board of directors unanimously decided to honor his memory by naming the administration building "The John A. Donahue Administration Building." The dedication ceremony was held September 29, 1985.

John A. Donahue

Group Homes

From June of 1978 through February of 1982, Hanna Center operated three off-campus group homes located in Napa, Petaluma and Santa Rosa. These homes were designed to meet the needs of boys who had successfully completed their courses at Hanna Center's main campus.

These boys needed supervision, guidance and an opportunity for developing independence, in a family-type living environment. They also needed involvement with society in ways that otherwise would not have been available to them. The group home residents lived with house parents and had regular contact with Hanna staff members. They attended local schools and took part in community activities in preparation for assuming purposeful and satisfying roles in their adult lives.

The boys were involved in school activities, and their names could be found on scholastic honor rolls, in cast lists for theatrical productions, and on sports teams' rosters. They were members of local Boys' Clubs, held jobs in their communities, and visited bowling alleys and movie theaters. They also spent their time doing household chores, studying, going to dances and traveling in the area with their friends.

House parents were married couples, and each house had relief workers who enabled them to take time off. Mr. John Reilly was the caseworker assigned to work with the boys and house parents of the group homes; he checked in several times each week at the homes to confer with the adults and the boys. Monsignor O'Connor and Father Pulskamp made frequent visits to keep aware of household events and residents' progress. Likewise, the boys were frequent visitors to the main campus, so they maintained close ties to the Center.

ORIE DAMEWOOD

Napa Group Home, 1910 First Street, opened September 9, 1968.

Top: Petaluma Group Home, 47 Sixth Street, opened September 9, 1968.

Bottom: Santa Rosa Group Home, 1451 Slater Street, opened December 3, 1969.

Toward the end of the 1970s, the number of boys who needed continued placement after completion of the Hanna curriculum decreased. Consequently, operation of the group homes became increasingly uneconomical, and gradually they were phased out and the houses sold. The Petaluma home closed in January of 1977, and the Napa home closed after the June graduation of 1978. The Santa Rosa home continued operating until February of 1982.

Two residents of the Napa group home during this era were Tom Lohwasser and Tom Chin. Both boys attended Justin-Siena High School and continued their education through college and graduate school. Examples of the success of the off-campus group home program, both men went on to have successful business and professional careers, meaningful family lives, contribute to their communities—and eventually return to Hanna as members of the Center's board of directors.

Hanna Boys Center has always measured its success by the achievement of its graduates. Tom Lohwasser and Tom Chin demonstrate that the group home program was a worthwhile endeavor.

Thomas Lohwasser, alumnus

Thomas Lohwasser, who described himself as "bewildered and somewhat angry" when he came to Hanna Boys Center in March of 1966, has devoted his career as a teacher and school administrator to helping youth, and he continues to maintain ties with Hanna Boys Center as a member of the board of directors.

Tom was a student at Hanna from March of 1966 until August of 1969, when he became a resident of Hanna's group home in Napa and attended Justin High School. Dr. Lohwasser said his time at Hanna provided him with the inspiration he needed to succeed.

"Hanna Center let me know that I was worth something," he said. "The Center gave me the initial opportunity to get back on the right track, to recognize that I had some potential and to lead a life that was aiming toward success, fulfillment, and happiness."

After graduating from Justin in 1973, he attended Santa Clara University, graduating in 1977, and then went on to earn his master's degree at the University of San Francisco in 1980 and his Ph.D. from LaVerne University, in La Verne, California in 1993.

After graduating from Santa Clara, he taught history and coached at St. Mary's Residence School for Boys in Napa. Tom progressed rapidly

at St. Mary's, and was named its first lay principal in July of 1981.

He was appointed superintendent of the Dixie School District in San Rafael, Marin County, in 1996. Upon his appointment, a written statement by the Dixie school board said, "Dr. Lohwasser has shown initiative, energy, enthusiasm, dedication, and a willingness to promote the best interest of the district as a whole. His outstanding administrative and team-building skills, his ability to work collaboratively with teachers, staff, and community members, and above all else, his credo, 'Is this good for the kids?' will serve this district well."

Tom and his wife Donna were married in the Hanna Center chapel in 1988. Their son Michael was born in 1991.

In addition to working with and for youth in his career, Dr. Lohwasser has been a member of Hanna Boys Center's board of directors, and frequently volunteers on campus to help with alumni events and special board meetings.

Above: Tom Lohwasser at his induction to the Hanna Board of Directors. From left: Bishop John T. Steinbock, Lou Geissberger, Tom Lohwasser, Robert Rossi and Father John Crews.

Right: Tom as a Hanna student.

School Principals

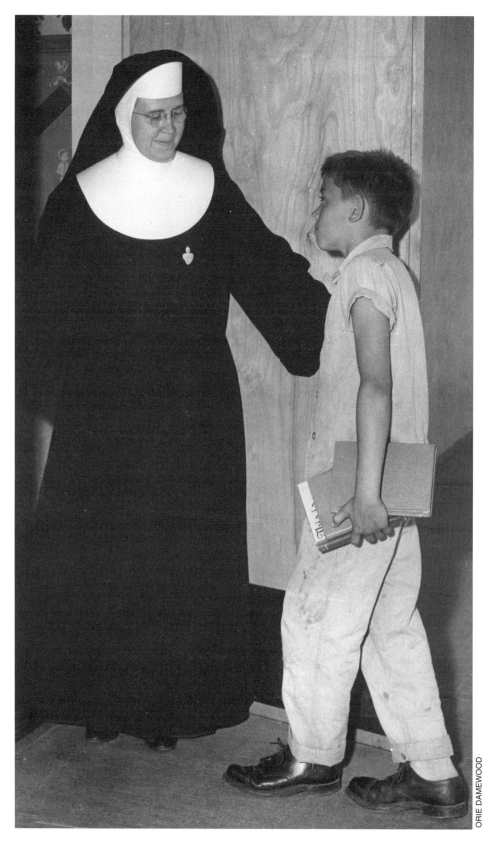

Dolores Jaehrling (see profile)
1968–76.

Chester Sharek
1976–79.

Robert McInnis
1979–87.

Left: Sister Mary Grace
1950–67.

Dolores Jaehrling

Dolores Jaehrling was born September 14, 1928, in South Milwaukee, Wisconsin. She attended St. Mary's Grade School, taught by the Sisters of St. Francis, and then went to the public high school in her hometown. Later, she completed two years at the University of Wisconsin Extension Division in Milwaukee. In 1948, her family moved to California.

Ms. Jaehrling worked for three years at the telephone company in Burlingame before deciding to join the Sisters of St. Francis. In 1951, as part of her training as a senior novice, Ms. Jaehrling was sent to Chicago to teach first grade, and in the following two years, 5th and 6th grades. Upon making her final profession of vows as a Sister of St. Francis, she received the name of Sister Carmel Therese. During this time she attended Cardinal Stritch College, now a university, and obtained her bachelor's degree in 1959. Later she continued her education at Loyola University in Los Angeles, where she obtained her master of arts degree in education.

In 1957, Sister Carmel Therese was assigned the duty of teaching summer school at Hanna Center—and was pleasantly surprised by the individualized attention the boys received. At the end of the summer, she was assigned to stay on permanently as a teacher at Hanna.

"That's when I thought I died and went to heaven," she recalled. "I had come from a large classroom in Milwaukee. My first class at Hanna had 10 boys and I wondered where the rest of them were." She soon discovered that she immensely enjoyed working with the boys and helping them meet their educational goals.

For eight years Sister Carmel Therese taught 7th and 8th grades at Hanna Center, covering all subjects in a self-contained classroom. In 1965, she was reassigned at the motherhouse in Milwaukee to be the director of novices. In 1968, she left the community and returned to Burlingame, California.

However, it wasn't long before Hanna Center came calling again, and she was invited to fill the vacant position of school principal in January of 1968. She served as principal of Hanna Center School until August of 1976, when she decided to return to the classroom. Ms. Jaehrling continued her service to the boys of Hanna by teaching religion, math, language arts, social studies and eventually computer assisted instruction. For many years she served as moderator for the school yearbook, stamp club coordinator and photo club moderator; she also wrote and published plays for student performances at the Center.

Shortly before her retirement in 1992, Ms. Jaehrling again took on the task of filling in as interim principal of the Hanna school while the principal was on medical leave.

Ms. Jaehrling has remained active with the Center's alumni association, and continues her life of service to others as a volunteer member of the board of directors of the Vintage House senior center in Sonoma.

Steve Cederborg 1987–97.

Bob Kruljac (left), 1998–99, and Carol Dillon, 1997–98.

James Hiss 1999–present.

No picture available: Sister Olive, principal, June–August, 1967.

James Schultz, music teacher

James Schultz

As the music instructor at Hanna Boys Center for nearly three decades (1964–93), Jim Schultz saw himself not just as a teacher of musical instruments, but as a partner in the development of the boys: teaching, understanding, and helping.

"I get a sense of satisfaction seeing the kids achieve," he said. "You can't help all of them, but if you can help one kid, it's worth it."

During his tenure at Hanna Boys Center, which culminated in his retirement at the age of 61 after the 1993 spring concert, Mr. Schultz presided over a 20-member band comprised of Hanna students playing all manner of instruments. About 90 percent of the band members had no instrumental experience before coming to Hanna, and Mr. Schultz would give each student a 40-minute private class each week in addition to group rehearsals. Participation was completely voluntary, and students could pick the instrument they wanted to play and switch if they became unhappy with it.

"I like to work with them one-on-one as much as possible, because it allows me to attend to the needs of each student," Mr. Schultz said. "Learning to do something and do it well really builds their self-esteem, especially for the ones who stick with it—they have the opportunity to see

themselves doing things they couldn't do before. They're able to read music off the sheet and make a contribution to the band—which means a lot to them."

A bassoon player his entire adult life, Mr. Schultz started playing the unique woodwind quite by accident—or luck. "I played the clarinet as a youngster, and when I got drafted, I played in the Presidio Army Band," Mr. Schultz remembered. "Their bassoonist was sent overseas and I was chosen as his replacement. Needless to say, I learned very quickly. It was that or be sent overseas myself."

After World War II, Mr. Schultz finished his education at the University of Southern California. He then went to Vienna, Austria, to begin "seriously" studying the bassoon. He played for the state opera there, and upon his return to the U.S., he played with the San Francisco, Oakland and the Santa Rosa symphony orchestras.

Mr. Schultz came to Hanna in 1964 and considered his tenure there an ideal career. "I've had the opportunity to do exactly what I want to do. I love music, I love teaching, and I love working with the boys here," he said, adding, "I did play professionally before coming here, but that wasn't nearly as rewarding as it has been to pass on my joy for music. It's wonderful to see kids coming out of rehearsal whistling a tune they just learned."

Today, Mr. Schultz continues to live in Santa Rosa with his wife Lucia, and the Hanna Center band, now under the direction of Jenifer Carstensen, continues to imbue students with a love of music and learning.

Opposite, right: Mr. Schultz at the Spring Concert.

Left: Mr. and Mrs. O. K. Jones and Father O'Connor with an early Hanna band.

Below: Hanna Boys Center marching band.

James E. Muldoon, public relations director

James E. Muldoon

James E. Muldoon, a tousle-haired gentleman of Irish descent with a warm personality and great sense of humor, could well be identified as the first person to "put Hanna Boys Center on the map" during his 32 years as the Center's first public relations director. Born March 9, 1919, in Kansas City, Missouri, he graduated in 1941 from Creighton University in Omaha, Nebraska, where he was a business major, with a minor in journalism.

That he preferred the latter was evident by the amount of time he devoted to writing for the school paper and serving as yearbook editor. In 1942, shortly after the U.S. became involved in World War II, Mr. Muldoon joined the Army and was commissioned a second lieutenant in the infantry. Prior to being shipped overseas, he married Cicely King, his college sweetheart.

A rifle company commander in the war against Nazi Germany, he took part in the 1944 invasion of Normandy at Omaha Beach. He was badly wounded at the battle of St. Lo and was awarded the Bronze Star, Purple Heart and Combat Infantry Badge.

In 1946, Mr. Muldoon began his civilian career working for Father Flanagan of Boys Town in Omaha, Nebraska, in public relations. In 1949 he decided to take advantage of the G.I. bill to further his education, heading west to enroll in the University of San Francisco's law school.

Shortly thereafter, deciding that the field of law was not for him, Mr. Muldoon accepted an offer to become Hanna Boys Center's first public relations director, in 1950. Father Flanagan personally recommended

him for the job at the relatively new "Boys Town of the West" in Sonoma, California, a post in which he successfully served from 1950 to 1982.

It was Mr. Muldoon who, in 1950, first recommended installation of a modified "Boys Town" direct mail fund-raising system for Hanna Center, supplemented by publicity efforts within the mailing area, which opened the door to bequests. This effort was the foundation of the successful funding and investment portfolio program still in existence today. Subsequently, the decision was made to remain free of any government funding so that the Center could maintain its program based on religious practices and values.

Mr. Muldoon enjoyed bantering with the boys on the Hanna campus, and looked upon founding

director Monsignor William L. O'Connor as the "most gentlemanly and caring" prelate he had ever known. With his engaging personality and sharp wit, Mr. Muldoon became a favorite visitor to newspaper offices, radio and television stations up and down the coast of California, singing the praises of Hanna Boys Center and dropping off photos and feature stories about the Center, which most promised to use—and did.

Herb Caen, the late San Francisco Chronicle columnist, occasionally ran items sent to him by Mr. Muldoon, who also won the respect of top entertainment and professional sports personalities, who sent autographed photographs for the boys or visited Hanna Center personally.

Through Mr. Muldoon's efforts, notables such as Joe DiMaggio, Bob Hope, Charleton Heston and Steve Allen recorded radio public service announcements on behalf of the boys and the Center. DiMaggio also visited the Center and spoke to the boys, as did California Governor Ronald Reagan, later President of the United States.

Mr. Muldoon recalled the late, great vocalist Nat "King" Cole as being "one of the nicest celebrities" he had ever met. Just before his death, Cole taped a public service announcement for Hanna Boys Center, but it was decided, in respect to his passing, not to use it.

Mr. Muldoon also reminisced occasionally about meeting George Burns (who gave him a cigar) and Gracie Allen, the famous comedy team, and singer Tennessee Ernie Ford.

Some of the many photographs of celebrities displayed on the walls of the Hanna Center administration building are a testament to Mr. Muldoon's contacts with top show business and sports figures who became Hanna boosters.

Mr. Muldoon got to know people who promoted major boxing matches and talked them into putting on benefit fights, with the proceeds going to Hanna Boys Center. Carl (Bobo) Olsen and Fred Apostoli were among the top boxers involved in those bouts.

Mr. Muldoon was also a frequent customer of two famous San Francisco restaurants—the Buena Vista Café and Ed Moose's Washington Square Bar and Grill—where he made many contacts who became supporters of Hanna Center.

In addition to serving at Hanna, Mr. Muldoon was a trustee of the Sausalito School District, a member of the Sausalito Parks and Recreation Commission, the Sausalito Schools Foundation, the San Francisco Press Club, the San Francisco Public Relations Round Table, the board of directors of St. Anthony's Dining Room; and a member of the Star of the Sea Catholic Church of Sausalito.

He died December 12, 1996, at the age of 77. His wife Cicely, still a resident of Sausalito, survives him, as do four of their five sons and two daughters, of whom he was very proud.

Opposite page, top: James E. Muldoon (photo courtesy of Mrs. James Muldoon).

Opposite page, bottom: Lou Costello and Bud Abbott work their "Who's on first?" routine on Hanna boy, 1950.

Left: Tennessee Ernie Ford with Hanna boys, 1964.

Above: Jim Muldoon (second from right) and Hanna boys with TV personality Herb Shriner.

Assistant Directors Who Served Hanna Center

Left: Father Gerald F. Cox, assistant director, 1958–62, pictured with movie star Pat O'Brien and two Hanna boys.

Bottom left: Father John O'Hare, assistant director, 1962–68.

Below top: Father Matthew Costello, Hanna social worker, 1986–89.

Bottom right: Father Gregory A. Klaas, assistant director, 1968–69.

No photo available: Father James Barry, who served in the Menlo Park faciility in 1945.

Attrition and change

Among the changes Father Pulskamp presided over, few were more poignant than the waning presence of the Sisters of St. Francis on the Hanna Boys Center campus. Most American religious communities were witnessing a drastic drop in vocations to the religious life, and since 1968, the number of sisters at Hanna Boys Center had begun to diminish. It soon became evident that when sisters died, retired or left the community there would be few replacements.

The hiring of lay teachers began in 1953, and as years progressed, they outnumbered the sisters. Through the 1970s, there were, on the average, eight sisters still living and working at Hanna. Some were semi-retired but continued to teach, taking small groups or tutoring individuals.

Sister Aloysine with student.

Though their numbers were diminishing, the sisters were still very visible and their influence remained strong. The sisters' lives were devoted to service, and the recipients of this service were always the boys; the primary goal was to provide an atmosphere of love and concern in every area in which the sisters worked. Attention was focused on each individual boy and his unique needs or problems, so as to encourage him to realize his full potential.

In 1971, Sister Romuald, another former mother general of the community, came to Hanna and worked as a caseworker. In 1974, at the request of Monsignor O'Connor, Sister Mary Peter helped form the alumni association. Along with her teaching religion classes full time, she worked diligently with the former boys, now men, who became members of this group.

The following decade appeared to be the beginning of the end of an era. After 30 years at Hanna Boys Center, Sister Mary Clare, one of the original sisters, died on February 1, 1980. In 1984, due to ill health, it was necessary for Sister Mary Grace, another original staff member, to return to the motherhouse. That same year, Sister Aloysine, also in poor health, left the Center after 20 years of service, followed by Sister Edwardine a few years later.

Sister Mary Clare, *teacher*

Sister Mary Clare

Sister Mary Clare was one of the original Sisters of St. Francis to arrive at Hanna Boys Center in 1949. Little did she know in those beginning days that she would be there for 30 consecutive years. But it was love at first sight when she saw the first boys arrive from Menlo Park; she knew teaching those boys was not going to be an easy task, but Sister Mary Clare was a veteran teacher and she relied on her years of experience.

Born in Mushawaka, Indiana, Sister Clare was well acquainted with the fame of her favorite football team, the "Fighting Irish" of Notre Dame. South Bend was just a few miles from her hometown. Often during her years at Hanna, Sister Clare would come to lunch chuckling over the fact that the boys were impressed that she knew so much about football. One day she told the sisters, "They couldn't believe I knew about Knute Rockne and that his team was the first to use the forward pass extensively. Of course I didn't tell them I had heard it when I was watching the game last week."

Many staff members who came to know her through the years were impressed with Sister Mary Clare's quiet, unassuming but cheerful mannerisms and her friendly way of inquiring how they were doing and how their families were.

All through her years at Hanna, Sister Clare taught 8th grade boys. Though discipline problems often arose, she had a quiet but very firm way of stemming off a disruption. Sometimes one look was all it took to quell the problem. She had great respect for each boy and her love and concern brought great respect for her.

Sister Mary Clare died February 1, 1980. In the yearbook, the boys remembered her on the In Memoriam page with these words: "For 30 years you greeted us as we came down from the cottages. When the last bell rang, you'd say, in your soft-spoken voice, 'Take your places, boys.' You were patient, you were kind and you taught us how to live and how to love. Now, you are in another world. And somehow, just maybe, when the last bell rings to call us where you are, we'll hear your gentle voice again, saying, 'Take your places, boys.'"

Sister Cordelia, nurse

Sister Cordelia was born in Milwaukee, Wisconsin, on August 18, 1905. She became a Catholic in 1922 at the age of 17. She entered religious life on August 14, 1926. In 1934, Sister Cordelia received her bachelor of science degree and nursing credentials from St Joseph's Hospital in Milwaukee. She served as a nurse in many locations before coming to Hanna Boys Center in August of 1960.

Sister Cordelia was delighted with the Center's newly constructed infirmary, completed in 1960. She eagerly took on the task of being in charge of this facility, seeing to it that health and dental care were systematically provided at the Center. She spent long hours nursing boys, working on records, restocking supplies and scheduling doctors' and dental appointments both on and off campus. She was highly skilled at what she did.

When there were no patients, Sister Cordelia could often be found working in the garden that gradually grew on the grounds of the infirmary. She had the proverbial green thumb and loved planting flowers. She often claimed that her flowers grew because she talked to them. Besides talking to her plants, she also talked to her pet parakeet, teaching him phrases such as "God bless you" and "I love you." No boy was capable of teaching Blueboy any swear words, although Sister Cordelia claimed she often caught some lad attempting to do it.

If a room was needed for a guest at the Center, Sister Cordelia was the perfect hostess and took great effort in making whoever came comfortable and at home. In fact, due to her care and hospitality, the infirmary was often referred to as The Cordelia Hilton. She saw to it that the rooms were spotless. It was not difficult for her to get boys to help her to keep it that way. They knew that after polishing and buffing floors or washing windows, Sister Cordelia would be very generous with some tasty treat that she always managed to coax from the sisters in the kitchen.

Sister Cordelia truly loved Hanna Boys Center. She made many friends in Sonoma, and doctors and dentists alike admired her greatly for her nursing skills. Many were sad to see her retire in

Sister Cordelia

1982. She returned to St. Ann's Health Center, located on the motherhouse grounds in Milwaukee. There she kept busy making her elderly sisters comfortable with another skill she had acquired, that of podiatry.

Sister Cordelia died March 5, 1993, at the age of 87. Today the many trees, bushes and flowers that surround the infirmary are a living testimony to this sister who loved nursing and nature. There is a quiet spot near the entrance where a birdhouse can be seen. On it is the inscription, "In Memory of Sr. Cordelia."

Father John S. Crews encircled by Hanna boys.

CHAPTER 4

The Crews Years
1984–present

Enhancing the Dream

The three directors: Monsignor O'Connor (seated at left), Monsignor Pulskamp (top right) and Father Crews (top left), pose with Bishop Hurley (seated at right) and Chairman of the Board of Directors Fred R. Grant (center).

When the Reverend Father John Crews came to Hanna Boys Center in 1984 he had the advantage of receiving guidance from his two predecessors, Monsignor O'Connor and Monsignor Pulskamp. When Father Crews became director of the Center, he had the challenge of establishing his management style and implementing his ideas for enhancing the program while the founder, Monsignor O'Connor, a living legend, was looking over his shoulder. Father Crews' humility, low-key approach and his consensus-seeking management style allowed him to accomplish his goals in a smooth, progressive transition while maintaining the basic values and goals of the Center.

Father Crews' directorship has been characterized by increased openness, greater inclusion of diverse opinions and increased opportunities for boys and families to realize success.

Father Crews' style of management is characterized by giving respect and dignity to boys and staff. When boys come to him with problems, he takes their problems seriously and treats them in a straightforward manner. When a staff member comes to him with a concern, he considers their viewpoint before making a decision. When staff members ask him to officiate at weddings, baptize their children, bless their marriages, speak at funerals or visit loved ones who are ill, he is flattered by their request and makes time on his busy schedule to conduct the spiritual ministrations. In this manner, Father Crews creates a family atmosphere at the Center. This culture of caring and respect for one another is a basic ingredient that fosters the healing of boys and families who come to the Center for help.

Father Crews is aware of the history of the Center. He often reminds the boys of Monsignor O'Connor's belief that each of us has to answer two questions before God at the end of our lives: "Did I do the best I could have with the talents I have been given?" and "Did I hurt anyone?"

The new director adopted a policy of getting the Center more involved in the community. The boys began participating in the Valley of the Moon Vintage Festival, Sonoma's Fourth of July parade, swimming with the Sonoma Sea Dragons, and competing as members of the local Babe Ruth Baseball League teams. He made the Center's facilities available to local soccer teams, swim teams, performing groups and clubs. Local parishes and churches have used the Center's grounds for carnivals and picnics.

Father Crews also wanted to increase the Center's contact with the boys after they left the program. He was instrumental in changing the by-laws of the alumni association to include all former students as members immediately after they left the Center. He encouraged former boys to visit the Center during open houses and family days, and he took an active role in the alumni association business meetings.

In addition, Father Crews assigned Father Matthew Costello to create and implement a follow-up program with the boys after they left the Center. A computerized system kept track of them and maintained their current addresses for newsletter and greeting card mailings, while an outcome measurement system evaluated the success rates of the graduates. Father Crews also broadened and increased the scholarship awards program, and he invited alumni members to serve on the Center's long-range planning committee.

During Father Crews' tenure, the physical plant and the enrollment at the Center have expanded. Two new group homes were built on campus to accommodate older boys who could attend the local high school. The Hanna school was granted accreditation by the Western Association of Schools and Colleges in March of 1991. The athletic field was landscaped. The convent building was converted to a cottage for 11 boys. All the cottages were remodeled, expanded and equipped with new furniture, and the recreation building and the kitchen were remodeled. An animal barn and a greenhouse were added, and a 4-H hog-raising program was instituted to allow boys who were interested to learn about animal husbandry.

Father Crews has named four school principals during his tenure: Steve Cederborg, Carol Dillon, Bob Kruljac and Jim Hiss. He enrolled the 2,000th and 2,500th boy into the program.

CHRIS BERGGREN

Father Crews is happiest in the chapel.

Father John S. Crews, director

Father John S. Crews

Encountering him on the Hanna Boys Center campus, one might get the impression that they were speaking with a mild-mannered country boy from the deep South. He might be dressed as a "civilian" in tennis shoes, a pair of khaki slacks and a sport shirt. One might notice a humble simplicity in mannerisms and speech. One might be fooled into thinking this is an unsophisticated man not conscious of his whereabouts nor focused on his mission.

Underneath this calm demeanor and unassuming personality, however, are the quick wit, keen intelligence, perceptive mind and complex personality of Father John S. Crews, the third director of Hanna Boys Center.

Father Crews was born April 8, 1945, to Sidney and Anne Crews, the eldest of four children. This son of an Army Air Corps pilot would perplex his father with a preference for the piano over airplanes and would become an accomplished classical pianist. Raised a Presbyterian, he would later perplex his father further with his preference for Catholicism.

John Crews graduated from Northeast High School in St. Petersburg, Florida, and after two years of study at the University of South Carolina, he converted to the Catholic faith and made the decision to enter the priesthood. He transferred to St. Mary's College Seminary in Baltimore, Maryland, where he earned a bachelor of arts degree in philosophy June 5, 1967. He continued his seminary studies at the Catholic University of America in Washington, D.C., where he earned a bachelor's degree in sacred theology February 26, 1970. He was ordained a priest February 14, 1971, in Washington, D.C. He continued his formal education at Catholic University, earning 30 graduate units in psychology.

Ever the adventurer, the young priest traveled to California. He was "claimed" by the bishop of Santa Rosa and assigned to parish work at St. Sebastian's in Sebastopol, where he served as associate pastor from August of 1971 through February of 1974. Father Crews continued his parish work at St. Joseph's in Cotati, where he was associate pastor from February of 1974, through May of 1980.

Finding himself more and more interested in the education of youth, Father Crews changed his vocational direction, serving as teacher and assistant principal at Cardinal Newman High School in Santa Rosa from May to December of 1980, and principal of St. Bernard High School in Eureka from December of 1980 through June of 1981. At the end of the school year he was assigned as diocesan director of religious education and youth ministry in Santa Rosa until December of 1983, when he became administrator pro-tem at St. Eugene's Cathedral in Santa Rosa. Finally, he was assigned the position of associate director of Hanna Boys Center January 1, 1984, and became director of the Center on July 1 of that year.

Father Crews continued his education at the University of San Francisco, earning a master's degree in education administration in December of 1980 and a doctor of education degree in educational psychology in the spring of 1989.

Father Crews holds a California Community College limited service teaching credential in humanities. He is also a commissioned officer in the United States Naval Reserve, chaplain, with the rank of captain. He has been a chaplain since 1977.

CHRIS BERGGREN

Chances are that you will not encounter Father Crews walking alone on the Hanna campus. Most often he has five or six boys tugging on his clothing, poking him in the ribs, pulling on his arms, hanging on his neck or draping themselves on his car trying to get that extra attention they crave. "I love it. I really do. The boys make it worthwhile," Father Crews said.

Not a man who enjoys administrative details or meetings, Father Crews spends most of his time where he thinks he can do the most good—with the boys and the boys' families. He personally interviews each boy and family prior to their acceptance in the program, and he forms a contract with both boy and family on the first day of the boy's admission, giving and receiving a formal commitment to the Center and the boy's pledge of working toward success.

"I see Hanna as a temporary helping place for a family. It's really sort of a 'time out' place when the boy needs to be away. The real challenge is to get the family to change. The boy didn't create the whole problem and doesn't have the responsibility for the whole change," he said.

Father Crews' leadership includes knowing personally the exact level of progress of every boy during his stay at Hanna. "I tell each of the boys that the goal from the first time you step in here is to go back home. In a way, go back to a new family that has expanded its horizons." He finds various ways of connecting with the boys, especially by taking them out for pizza on their birthdays, jogging with them in the evenings, attending their sports competitions, musical recitals, and graduations, and handing out report cards.

He maintains an open-door policy during office hours and will answer his door at home when a boy comes to him in crisis late at night. Even after the boys have completed their stay and left the Center, he returns their phone calls and letters.

Father Crews is the representative of Christ at Hanna Boys Center. He is quick to remind all that "ultimately it is the power of God that untangles the confusion, enlightens the doubts, and heals the wounds of our boys and their families." He has continued the work of his predecessors, Monsignor O'Connor and Monsignor Pulskamp, and he has kept the values of Hanna Center alive and at the forefront of the learning and service that is offered the boys each day.

Father Crews and cast of boys about to videotape a greeting for the Annual Golf Classic.

NED DAVIS

"Hanna Boys Center is a far better place thanks to Bob Seymour," said Father John Crews, executive director of Hanna. "Every department at the Center has been influenced by Bob's caring concern for the boys and the Center. He will never be forgotten by those who knew him and of his many contributions to the Center."

Robert C. Seymour

Born in Vallejo, California, Mr. Seymour grew up in San Francisco, where he graduated from Polytechnic High School. He remembered fondly his sports career there and was quick to remind people of his athletic prowess. A skilled baseball player, Mr. Seymour was offered a spot with a touring professional team, but his father would not allow his young son to forego his education.

Baseball's loss was the San Francisco School District's and Hanna Boys Center's gain. Mr. Seymour graduated from San Francisco State University, took graduate studies at Stanford and received his master's degree from San Francisco State.

After a tour with the U.S. Navy during World War II, Bob began a distinguished educational career in San Francisco that spanned 34 years. Before joining Hanna Boys Center as director of finance and administration in 1984, Mr. Seymour served as a teacher for many years and as director of personnel for the San Francisco Unified School District for 16 years. He was an esteemed consultant to school districts throughout the United States.

Mr. Seymour served the Center in a number of capacities: his first contact was as a generous benefactor, then as a dedicated volunteer board member. In 1984, he accepted the position of director of finance and administration—a post he held for 12 years. After his retirement in 1996, he again became a member of Hanna's board of directors.

An ardent golfer, Mr. Seymour was among the founders of the Annual Hanna Boys Center Benefit Golf Classic, along with his late friend, Noel Mertens. Among Mr. Seymour's qualities were his compassion for others and his quest to provide the boys with the best education and treatment possible. Through his own generous donation, he established the Robert C. Seymour Educational Fund that provides ongoing financial aid to deserving Hanna graduates seeking higher education.

At an annual Hanna board meeting, one director praised Mr. Seymour, calling him "the world's greatest administrator." Mr. Seymour possessed a low-key manner of putting people at ease that allowed him to solve difficult personnel problems and to resolve potential conflicts before they even arose. Many staff members sought Mr. Seymour's advice on career plans, program matters or personal questions. Mr. Seymour was a great listener who gave everyone who came into contact with him the impression that they were the most important subject in the world at that particular moment.

While at Hanna, Mr. Seymour was a member of the Rotary Club of Sonoma Valley and served as club president in 1988. He was also a past president of the Peacock Gap Country Club, Phi Delta Kappa, Bay Area School Personnel, Large California School Districts and Marin County Special Olympics. Mr. Seymour died at his home in San Rafael on June 7, 1998. His wife Virginia survives him and has since represented him on the Hanna board of directors.

Mr. Seymour and Father Crews formed a close working alliance soon after they met at Hanna. Forming an unbeatable team, they complemented one another, allowing each to concentrate on the aspects of the job that they did best. The result was a smooth-working management team characterized by sound decisions and compassion for staff, boys, and families.

Father Crews wished to honor Mr. Seymour and his contributions to Hanna Center in a special way. Accordingly, he decided to add Mr. Seymour's name to the dedication plaque of the administration building. The building is now known as "The Robert S. Seymour and John A. Donahue Administration Building."

Program Highlights

During his 15-year tenure, Father Crews has changed the style of the Hanna program, allowing the staff more direct involvement in the boys' treatment and in the decision-making process. Believing that no one person has the full knowledge to make a decision about a boy's future, he listens to many opinions before he makes his decisions. He has developed procedures for formalizing suspension hearings and discipline review boards.

Another innovation has been the creation of guided group interaction, wherein trained staff members meet with boys in a safe forum to give the boys the opportunity to express their feelings and learn social skills. Ken Krumdick, a veteran of over 40 years as a child care worker at Hanna, said, "The group process has been the best innovation for treatment since I have been here."

In 1986, Father Crews personally selected Tim Norman, Ph.D., to serve as psychologist for the Center. Dr. Norman's straightforward, common sense approach to therapy melded nicely with the caring, personal-style atmosphere Father Crews advocated for the Center.

Father Crews is renowned for his compassion in giving boys second, third, and fourth chances to return to the program and make a success of their enrollment. He firmly believes that if a boy stays in the program for only one day, that boy will have gained something from his experience at Hanna. In this way, he views every boy who comes to Hanna as a gift from God and he views every boy's experience at the Center as valuable.

CHRIS BERGGREN

24-year Hanna staff veteran Greg Clefisch facilitates a group process session in one of the cottages.

Ken Krumdick, *child care worker*

"I always knew what I wanted to do," said Ken Krumdick while reflecting on more than 47 years as a child care worker. "I wanted to teach youngsters, and Hanna Center offered me the opportunity to do exactly that."

Kenneth Krumdick

Ken was born and raised in Manitowoc, Wisconsin, an area he described as "dairy country." The son of a dairy rancher and a schoolteacher, he is the second oldest in a family of two boys and three girls.

Ken got his start working in residential treatment during his college years, when he worked at Mission of Our Lady of Mercy school for boys in Chicago. Upon earning his degree in philosophy from Loyola University in Chicago, Ken moved to California, where he discovered Hanna Boys Center through an employment agency.

"I was amazed when I saw the campus," Ken remembered. "It was beautiful. Father O'Connor checked my references in Chicago and he asked me if I could start work the next day. So I did. That was in 1956. We were assigned as one staff for 20 boys. The salary was $200 per month. It was nothing to work 70 to 80 hours each week. We just did it because we had to do it. There was no one else to do the work. I lasted over 40 years because I'm strong-willed and I have always been able to separate what was important from what was not important. Being with young boys gives me vitality and makes me feel good, too. Most of the boys I worked with have been good kids. There were a few who couldn't take advantage of the second chance Hanna offered them; I feel sorry for them."

Possessing a good sense of humor and quick to laugh, Ken infused a positive attitude into the atmosphere of the cottage. Many boys enjoyed his chatter during his famous croquet games. His positive regard for the boys gave them the confirmation that they were important to him. Ken's attention to detail in all facets of cottage life taught the boys that everything they did was worthwhile. His high standards for cleanliness, orderliness, observation of manners and courtesy and rule enforcement set a standard for his staff and for the child care workers in other cottages.

Never married, Ken has dedicated his life work to the boys of Hanna Center. "Hanna has been like my home," he stated. "I just enjoyed being here and working with the boys."

Many former boys who come back to visit the Center ask, "Is Mr. Krumdick still here?" Yes, Mr. Krumdick is still here, enjoying himself and teaching boys how to become better persons.

John Reilly, Father Crews, Sister Peter, Dee Jaehrling and Ken Krumdick at 1997 Jim Healy Memorial Field Day.

Departure of the Sisters of St. Francis

When school opened in the fall of 1990, there were no nuns living at Hanna Boys Center for the first time in 40 years. The Sisters of St. Francis, who had taught the boys of Hanna since the Center was established in 1949, had left the previous July.

Three of the four sisters who remained in early 1990 had left the Center for other assignments. Sister Mary Peter and Sister Mary Immaculate returned to the motherhouse in Milwaukee, Wisconsin, while Sister Joan moved to the Ursuline Convent in Santa Rosa and nursing duties at St. Vincent's Hospital in San Rafael. Sister Ruth changed her residence to a convent at Justin-Siena, in Napa, and continues to work at Hanna as teacher, sacristan and campus minister. She also assists in coordinating alumni events at the Center.

Throughout the 1980s, the convent at Hanna Boys Center had emptied, and the building was finally converted into a residence for

Sisters of St. Francis with Bishop Maher and Monsignor O'Connor circa 1962.

From left: Sisters Yvonne Therese, Cordelia, Grace, Virgine, Philomene, Alberta, Carmel Therese, Clare, Mona, Elizabeth, Allen Marie and Anna Marie (in white).

boys—aptly named St. Francis Cottage, in honor of the patron saint and the sisters who spent so many dedicated years on the Hanna campus.

Sister Mary Peter, who upon departure in 1990 had given 30 years of service at Hanna, called the plan to turn the convent into a residence cottage for the boys a "bittersweet decision." But since she and Sister Mary Immaculate were retiring, it seemed like a good time for the school to make the change, she said.

"The sisters' absence will be a major transition for the Center, because they have been here since the first day. In fact, the doors didn't even open until everything was to the sisters' liking," said Father Crews.

"Along with the discipline, education, love and dedication these sisters shared with their charges at Hanna Boys Center, they also helped with the boys' spiritual growth," said Father Crews. "Their real strength has been their teaching, discipline and the way the boys loved them," he added.

Consistently, the sisters and faculty had been available for round-the-clock attention whenever the boys needed to talk. "Monsignor O'Connor always told me that state institutions can feed them, house them and entertain them, but we had to give them the added dimension of a religious education," Sister Peter said.

Celebration of Holy Mass, a reception and a brunch were held on campus to honor the sisters and to mark the occasion of their departure. Faculty members, staff and many former boys attended the event to pay tribute to the sisters. Amusing stories were retold and a plethora of happy memories were recalled during the festivities.

Sister Ruth working with a Hanna student at the computer.

Though there is no longer a convent on campus, the prayers of the sisters continue to be expressed for their boys—for students who arrived on the bus from Menlo Park in 1949 and for all those who came through the front gate during the following years. The sisters' prayers can best be summed up with the words etched in the glass window above the door that once led to the convent: "May the Lord bless you."

The Sisters of St. Francis left an indelible tradition of caring, education, hard work, and excellence at Hanna Boys Center. Their physical presence is gone, but their spiritual presence endures. After the sisters' departure, Father Crews established the campus ministry program to help fill the void left by their departure.

Sister Mary Peter, *teacher*

Ever since her first communion, Sister Mary Peter had the desire to be a nun. Her ambition was realized when she entered the convent in 1933. Always an excellent student, she worked diligently and obtained her bachelor's degree in English at Cardinal Stritch University and a master's degree in the same field at Lone Mountain, the San Francisco College for Women. At Mundelein College in Chicago, she obtained her certification in religious education.

When Hanna Center was less than a year old, Sister Peter arrived to teach Latin, English, algebra, biology and social studies in the high school division. She found the experience to be challenging, but she knew she was being effective and grew to love working with the boys.

She wanted very much to continue working at Hanna, but after 10 years, her religious superiors had other plans for her. In 1960, she was assigned to teach in North Carolina, and later in Mauston, Wisconsin, as a high school teacher and principal. From there she was sent to teach religion and Latin at St. Mary's Academy in Milwaukee. Though Sister Peter loved her work in all these places, her heart remained at Hanna Boys Center.

In 1970, much to Sister Peter's joy and Hanna Center's good fortune, at the request of Monsignor O'Connor, she returned to the Center to teach religion. Here her love continued to grow and her influence with the boys was evident. Sister Peter spent long hours preparing lessons that stimulated a boy's interest. She encouraged discussions and was always open to opinions and questions that were challenging.

Sister Peter remained at the Center for 20 more years, until 1990, when she returned to Clare Hall, a retirement home for the sisters, near the motherhouse in Wisconsin. But retirement is not a word that fits Sister Mary Peter. She spends many hours working and meeting the needs of her sick and infirm sisters at another facility several miles from where she lives.

Sister Mary Peter hears from many of "her boys," now men, who remember their days at Hanna and the love and guidance given by their beloved teacher.

When Sister Mary Peter left Hanna, the bishop of the diocese of Santa Rosa sent a letter that means much to her, and she hopes his words are true: "Through your teaching, many boys came to know and trust the Lord and to experience His

Sister Mary Peter

love... You have impacted not just one generation but many."

If Sister Mary Peter has any doubt of the truth of these words, there are countless former students who believe it firmly and carry the memory of her in their hearts.

On-Campus Group Homes

When Father Crews assumed responsibilities as director of Hanna Boys Center, he realized there was a need to provide a home on campus for boys who had successfully completed the main campus program. These were boys who did not have a viable home or family with which to reunite, or boys who needed additional time to mature and develop self-responsibility. These young men were generally junior- and senior-year high school students who would very likely earn their diplomas soon.

To meet this need, Father Crews initiated plans for a 12-bed house to be built on the main campus. By locating the home at Hanna, Father Crews planned that the group home program would benefit from the support systems already in existence in the main campus program. The young men of the new group home could take advantage of the facilities and staff expertise available to the boys in the Hanna program; at the same time, spiritual guidance and the chapel would be readily available to them.

The new group home was ready for operation on July 7, 1986. Eventually, the home was dedicated as the Father O'Connor House, in memory of the co-founder of the Center.

Initially, the boys in the group home attended either Justin-Siena High School in Napa or Sonoma Valley High School. In recent years, the boys have attended Sonoma Valley High School, Creekside High School or a combination of classes at Sonoma Valley schools and the Hanna Center School. This combination has provided the flexibility necessary for meeting the individual needs of each student. To assist the boys in their studies, tutors were made available at the group home in the evenings. The Hanna staff also met regularly with the boys' teachers to monitor progress, and worked very zealously to encourage the boys to remain motivated in their studies. The boys were also encouraged to become involved with extracurricular activities. Group home residents have been involved in drama, peer counseling, band, sports, and student body government.

The Father O'Connor House proved to be a successful program for this age group of Hanna students and paved the way for expansion as more young men graduated from the main campus program. A second group home, the Father Flanagan House, was built on campus and dedicated on December 4, 1991, in honor of the other co-founder of Hanna Boys Center. Monsignor Flanagan was present to dedicate both the Father O'Connor House and the dwelling named after himself on the 42nd anniversary of the opening of Hanna Boys Center in Sonoma.

First graduating class of the Father O'Connor Group Home, 1987.

Front row left to right: Pat Verdi, John Inthilatvongsy, Renzo Fidani, Mick Lazzarini, Steve Phavasiri.

Second row: Bill Van Aken, Ken Murphy, Chris Anderson, Erick McAllister, Jeff Kirk, Mike Williams.

Back row: Staff members Jack Guge, Bill Byrne, Lou Young, Carlos Jacobo, Richard Bourgeois and Bonnie Nelson.

The group home program was designed to provide an environment where young men could continue their growth into adulthood by offering them experiences similar to those of a typical family. The group home staff serves many of the functions of parents for youths who are rapidly growing into manhood. These trained professionals are guides, advisors, supervisors, and morale builders for the boys. The staff members live in rooms located in the group home while they are on duty. There are a total of four staff members, with two on duty at all times. One of the four staff members serves as the supervisor.

The entire Hanna Center program is built on the foundation of group living. At the group homes, as in every cottage on the main campus, every resident has his responsibilities in maintaining the home. These responsibilities include meal planning, shopping, cooking, laundry, and house cleaning. The boys and staff meet several times each week as a group to discuss any concerns that may arise.

Father Flanagan House, dedicated December 4, 1994.

In addition to attending the local public schools, the boys can hold part-time jobs in the community. They can also entertain their friends at the home, earn their driver's license and (with certain strict conditions) own a car, and have free time in town. They are learning what all young people have to learn in order to become mature adults—that is, to enjoy the privileges of earned confidence and to accept responsibility for their actions. In the growing process, they also develop needed self-esteem.

Participants in the group home program attend school dances, clubs, and parties where they learn how to interact with their peers. Socializing with girls is an important part of growing up, and both group and individual counseling are available from the staff to help meet the challenge.

To assist the boys in learning the skills they will need in order to live on their own, experts are invited to address the group on subjects such as the management of money, handling a checking account, establishing credit, and paying taxes. Other discussion topics include cooking skills, job interviews, filling out college applications, and vocational training.

For these boys who will move directly from the group home into the adult world, the focus is on offering as many opportunities as possible to learn the skills they will need to live on their own as responsible, independent young men.

Hanna is especially proud of the young men in the group home program, because they have risen to meet squarely the many challenges of their lives and are well on their way to becoming mature men who will make a positive contribution to society.

Noma Martini, alumnus

First Lieutenant Noma Martini.

played football and ran on the track team. His senior year he was student body vice president and valedictorian. Noma attended the University of California at Berkeley, where he joined the Army ROTC Program and a fraternity and worked as a cadet with the University Police Department. With financial assistance from the Hanna scholarship program, Noma graduated from college with a double major, history and American studies. Upon graduation, Noma was commissioned as a second lieutenant in the U.S. Army. Now First Lieutenant Martini is stationed at Fort Irwin, California, where he has served as an infantry platoon leader and is a company executive officer. Noma will realize his lifelong dream of becoming a pilot, as he has been selected to attend flight training school.

Noma shared a few thoughts about what Hanna Boys Center means to him. "Now that Hanna Boys Center has become a part of my life I feel that I will use many of the positive attributes of this program when raising my children. To teach them the respect, caring and faithfulness that Hanna Boys Center has helped me to develop within my own life."

Noma has returned to the Center to talk to the boys about military life and to let the staff know how they contributed to his success.

Noma as a Hanna student.

Born in Oakland, California, Noma Martini got off to a rocky start in life. The son of a single-parent mother, Noma lacked motivation in school and positive direction in his life. He had some minor brushes with the law. His mother sought a more positive environment for her son and discovered Hanna Boys Center.

Noma was 14 years old when he enrolled at Hanna, and he resided at the Center for 4-1/2 years from December of 1986 through June of 1991. He began his stay at Hanna in the cottages and later transferred to the group home. Noma attended Sonoma Valley High School, where he

Verna Moll, *librarian*

With a lifelong goal of providing every child she encountered with the skills to read and enjoy new books, Verna Moll dedicated over 27 years of her professional career to Hanna Boys Center as librarian.

Born June 16, 1924, in Los Angeles to Vern and Josephine Doane, Verna attended Garfield High School. She had two brothers, Chuck and Howard.

During World War II Verna worked at the McDonnell-Douglas airplane factory. Her brother Howard brought home on leave a fellow bombardier named John Moll. Verna and John fell in love and married shortly after the end of the war. The couple relocated to Sonoma where John's father was a leading building contractor. John succeeded him in that business here.

Mrs. Moll came to Hanna Center in September of 1969 and immediately began instilling students with a love of reading. "I sell reading. I work hard to get the boys to like reading, to want to read," she recalled. "Without reading skills, it's not possible to function well in life, go to school and get a high school diploma."

In addition to working with the boys, Mrs. Moll assisted donors to the Center in the establishment of special library funds to help ensure that the boys always had books and audiovisual materials to assist with schoolwork and for enjoyment.

Following her retirement in 1996, Mrs. Moll continued to live in Sonoma and focused on her love of writing. She also spent numerous hours gardening—and reading. She died October 12,1998, but the love of reading she instilled in her charges lives on.

CHRIS BERGGREN

Verna Moll

Sister Ruth, *teacher*

Sister Ruth was born in Mobile, Alabama, March 24, 1928. As a youngster, she had a natural aptitude for athletics. Her interest in this area caused her to major in physical education at the Montebello State Teachers College in her home state. Before finishing, she was hired to teach physical education in Los Altos Hills, California, in a school staffed by the Sisters of Charity. It was while there that she decided to enter the convent and chose the Sisters of St. Francis in Milwaukee. She entered the order on November 21, 1950. While a senior novice, Sister Ruth was sent to teach at St. Aemillian's School for Boys in Milwaukee. She was there for 12 years, one year as a 4th and 5th-grade teacher, and then, at her request, as a house mother so she could assist boys in the athletic program. She attended Cardinal Stritch College, now a university, and received her master's degree in education.

Sister Ruth's experience in working with youth includes four years at St. Coletta's School for Exceptional Children in Jefferson, Wisconsin, as well as nine years at the Joseph Kennedy School in Palos Park, Illinois. She came to St. John's in Napa in 1978 and taught 4th and 5th grades. While living in Napa, Sister Ruth often came to Hanna to visit the sisters and help around the convent. She became very interested in working with the boys and in 1983 was hired to become the 6th grade teacher. She worked in that area until 1990, when she became campus minister. In that position, Sister Ruth is the campus sacristan and continues to teach religion classes, instruct the altar boys, give lessons on the sacraments, plan liturgies, and to play a key role in the alumni events that are presented for the boys on campus.

Anyone who knows Sister Ruth is aware of her boundless energy. A former staff member and long-time friend teases her and fondly calls her "The Energizer Bunny."

Without a doubt, Sister Ruth's prayer life and her love and dedication to the work at Hanna are bound to help keep those batteries charged for a good long time.

Sister Ruth Gardner

BILL BYRNE

Into the Future

Father Crews has plans for an additional cottage to expand enrollment by 12 more boys. This will increase the Center's enrollment capacity to 119 boys. Plans are in place to add a new wing to the school that will create computer and science laboratories and a room for the music program. The dining hall will be renovated during the year 2000.

Also, there are plans for extending Hanna's services to a larger community. In conjunction with Catholic Charities in Santa Rosa, Hanna will be operating a "warm line" that is designed to respond to children who are home alone and want to talk with an adult. Hanna's caseworkers will offer parenting classes in local parishes and other community locations in the Bay Area. Father Crews has dreams of creating a separate facility for a girls' program to help meet the increasing needs of today's problem-ridden society.

Hanna Boys Center in the 1980s and 1990s has built on the solid foundation established by its founders. Under Father Crews' leadership the Center has remained true to the mission, goals and values that Monsignor O'Connor instituted 50 years ago and that Monsignor Pulskamp protected and nurtured through the 1970s. The Center enters the year 2000 with a sense of purpose and optimism—and with dreams: dreams of helping more boys. Dreams of expanding. Dreams of extending service to girls and their families. Dreams of excellence.

Boys wave hello from top of the sign at the campus main entrance.

DEE JAEHRLING

1977 Board Chairman and Director Emeritus Albert A. Maggini with boys.

CHAPTER 5

The Hanna Boys Center Community

Friends, Supporters and Volunteers

Hanna Boys Center has always relied on support and assistance from various community members. In the 1940s, parishioners and individual donors joined the volunteer Hanna board of directors in creating the Center. The individual donors and the volunteer board of directors have been constant sources of support for the Center ever since. As the Center strengthened itself through years of performance and achievement other sources of support developed to lend assistance.

Through the generous gifts of benefactors a scholarship program was developed to offer continuing educational benefits to the Center's graduates. The Center's graduates themselves have organized and have found ways to support the program and its boys. Other benefactors and volunteers have emerged to offer their services, skills and special support in numerous ways.

It is difficult to describe and detail, within the limits of this book, all of the people who have contributed in so many ways throughout the years. The following sections are intended to honor and to thank those who have been so generous to Hanna Boys Center.

The Scholarship Program

Underlying all work at Hanna Boys Center is the belief that God Himself has brought each student to the Center in order to receive guidance as he journeys toward adulthood. Hopefully, among the lessons boys learn while at the Center is that struggle and sacrifice are necessary to earn what is most valuable in life. A formal education is one of life's most valuable achievements, and struggle and sacrifice are inevitable in earning that education.

Pursuit of formal education has been from its beginning an essential part and a primary goal of the Hanna Boys Center program. In addition to providing schooling while residing at the Center, students are very strongly encouraged to continue their studies after leaving the on-campus program. Further learning opportunities for a student may include elementary or high school, college and university level education, or a work-training program.

To assist boys in this endeavor, a special fund was established in 1952 to ensure that graduates who qualified would be able to receive financial assistance as they continued their education. Over the years, Hanna has been able to offer financial assistance to hundreds of young men.

"The Sisters of St. Francis Scholarship Program" is named in honor of the sisters who served the Center for more than 50 years. Generous donors have established the Ray P. Paoli Trade School Trust Fund, the

Roy Willmarth Vocational Fund, the Robert Seymour Educational/ Scholarship Fund, the Kozel College Scholarship Fund, the Antonio G. Soletti General Fund, and the General Scholarship Fund, among others. The scholarship program has steadily expanded since 1952. In the last 10 years alone, 143 boys have received a total of more than $720,000— an average of $5,000 per boy.

To qualify for a scholarship, a boy must successfully complete the Hanna Boys Center program, demonstrate a desire to continue his education, complete a written application, and appear before the scholarship committee for an interview. The scholarship committee is comprised of several members of the Hanna board of directors' education and treatment committee. These professionals volunteer their services to interview, select and advise the scholarship recipients. They take a personal interest in the boys and keep in touch with them throughout the school year.

The results of the scholarship program have been excellent. Former Hanna students have successfully graduated from St. John's University, the University of California at Berkeley, Sonoma State University, Howard University, San Francisco State University, Chapman University, and Cal Poly at San Luis Obispo. In addition, the scholarship program has helped many young men obtain A. A. degrees from community colleges and diplomas from Catholic high schools. One former boy became an air conditioning technician supported by a scholarship grant. Another graduated from the Culinary Arts Institute in New York and is now a chef at the Waldolf Astoria Hotel in New York City. Several students have completed police and fire fighters' academies and are now serving their communities.

The Roy Willmarth Vocational Fund was established to honor the memory of the much loved woodshop teacher (shown above with some of his students in the classroom shop) by extending scholarship support to boys who wish to further their educations.

Former boys in the program currently attend Humboldt State University, San Francisco State University, San Francisco Academy of Arts, San Diego State University and the California State University at Stanislaus.

It is a wonderful thrill when the scholarship committee receives an invitation to commencement exercises from a young man in the Sisters of St. Francis Scholarship Program. The educational achievements of these young men justify and reward the generosity of the donors and the hard work of the Hanna staff and board of directors.

Earning diplomas represents one more step in these students' journey toward successful and productive lives.

Bill Conley, *alumnus*

Bill and Donna Conley with daughter Madeline Louise.

"Even from the very first day at Hanna, I knew that I was going to get the help I needed to become whole again." With these words, Bill Conley summarized his experience and the benefits he received from his relationship with Hanna Boys Center.

Now a happily married family man with a wife and daughter, Bill enjoys his demanding job as a member of the San Francisco Police Department. However, Bill's life did not start out on such a positive note.

The only child of a broken marriage, Bill was about six years old when his parents divorced. The marriage had been an unhappy and chaotic one, and the divorce was marked by bickering and a bitter custody suit. Bill decided that he wanted to live with his mother and they relocated from New York to San Francisco.

Bill's mother found it difficult being head of the family and a single parent. Bill did not react well to her erratic and inconsistent parenting style. He had a difficult time with authority figures at home and at school. He had little concept of time and could not accept responsibility for his actions. His mother sought help, placing Bill at Hanna Center.

When Bill first came to Hanna, he was one month shy of his 12th birthday. He displayed manipulative behavior, having difficulty differentiating between right and wrong. He was moody and his attitude fluctuated accordingly.

Soon, Bill began to involve himself in the Hanna program. He formed a solid relationship with his caseworker, with whom he was open about discussing his emotional issues. In school, he expressed a desire to succeed and to cooperate and became a high achiever. He enjoyed the physical training and sports program, where he was competitive and energetic.

Work became a good outlet for Bill, and he became a member of athletic teams, especially basketball; took guitar lessons; and was involved in almost all the activities open to him. He developed an ability to take directions and suggestions from staff as his self-confidence increased and his trust in adults deepened.

After three years at Hanna, Bill graduated from the eighth grade. His mother had remarried and the relationship seemed stable. The family had partaken of family counseling sessions at Hanna, and wanted Bill to come home. At graduation Bill was named the Boy of the Year.

With scholarship assistance from Hanna, Bill attended and graduated from Sacred Heart High School in San Francisco. The scholarship enabled him to continue his education at the University of San Francisco prior to joining the police academy.

Later, Bill reflected on the period of his life at Hanna. "Father Crews and the staff and boys at Hanna are my second family. I grew up, matured and persevered at Hanna. The board of directors and the scholarship committee recognized my deep desire to succeed and granted me scholarships to finish my education. I wouldn't be where I am today without the support and direction I received at Hanna Boys Center."

Bill returns frequently to visit the staff and boys. He has spoken at the annual board of directors meeting, and has given the benefit of his perspective to staff members at training sessions.

Bill Conley is a true inspiration to the boys and staff of Hanna Center. Working the night shift as a police officer in the Hunter's Point neighborhood of San Francisco is not easy, but Bill really enjoys it. His positive outlook, which he attributes to Hanna's teachings and guidance, helps him deal with the stress and the day-to-day problems he encounters. Bill focuses on all the good he can do for the people living, working and growing in the area, and he sincerely takes to heart the words "to protect and serve."

Right: Bill as a Hanna student.

Alumni Association

The motto of the Hanna Boys Center Alumni Association is "Amicus et Frater"—"friend and brother." For more than 25 years, the members of the alumni association have served as friend and brother to hundreds of students at Hanna and have supported one another through life-long friendships.

Monsignor William O'Connor held the first "Alumni Day" at Hanna Center on June 24, 1956. Thereafter, get-togethers were held periodically to renew old friendships and to allow former boys to see how the campus had changed. In his role as assistant director in the 1970s, Monsignor O'Connor sought to formalize an association of former boys, based on a philosophy of mutual support and service to the Center. In January of 1974, alumnus John Brown and his wife invited five Hanna staff members to dinner in their Belmont home to discuss plans for the formation of the organization. As a result, in May of that year Hanna caseworker John Reilly and Sister Mary Peter held an organizational meeting at the Hanna campus. Fifteen alumni, representing classes from 1948 through 1967, attended the meeting and listened to Monsignor O'Connor propose ideas for the formation of the organization.

Because of the enthusiasm and support the alumni expressed at the May meeting, a second gathering was scheduled for the following October to elect officers and create by-laws. At that meeting, John Brown was elected president, while Myron MacNeil and Frank Youngblood were chosen as vice-president and secretary, respectively. Committee members charged to charter the by-laws were John Wade '65, Al Carli '53, Harry Dillon '57, Al McCue '61 and Claude Maurer '63.

Charter meeting of the Alumni Association, May 18, 1974.

Front row from left: Mrs. Ann Healy, Sister Clare, Father O'Connor, Sister Grace, Sister Peter.

Middle row: Ralph Frietze, John Reilly, William Murphy, Norberto Anzano, Albert Carli, John Brown, David Lopez, Brian Choy and Reno Russo.

Back row: Terry Longacre, Frank Youngblood, Ed Stevens, Roger Harrison, Myron MacNeil and Albert Haggett.

COURTESY OF RAY DOHERTY

The purpose of the association, as formulated by those charter members, is to provide a means by which former boys keep in touch with and assist one another and aid the Center staff in helping younger boys take their places in the community as worthwhile, productive citizens.

Through the years, the alumni have gathered, not only at the Center for activities, but also off-campus for socials, picnics, funerals, christenings, weddings and sales. Members support one another by sharing job openings and offering job training, assisting one another with family projects, sustaining those in financial need, and sponsoring fund-raising projects such as garage and flea market sales, gathering and recycling aluminum cans, and recycling scrap metals.

Two activities in the association's early years included "Big-Brother Visiting"—phoning or writing boys who left the Hanna program and were in need of emotional support—and befriending Hanna boys who had no visitors during Visiting Sundays at the campus.

Since 1980, the association has sponsored the "Jim Healy Field Day"—named in honor of Hanna's first athletic director—conducting sports competitions and awarding trophies and T-shirts to boys who participate. Each spring, the association conducts the carnival for the

Ray Doherty (center), class of '50, with wife Teresa, children and grandchildren. Ray is a graduate of Texas A&I with a degree in industrial management. He is owner and manager of four companies serving the oil industry. He frequently sends cash donations for ice cream for the boys.

Opposite page, clockwise from top: John Brown ('60) on the left and Frank Youngblood ('59) mugging at an alumni dinner.

Frank and Dorothy Youngblood at home in Snohomish, Washington. They were married in the Hanna chapel.

Ken Larsen, DDS ('55) and family. Ken is a dentist in Minneapolis.

Tom Lohwasser ('73) and Sister Ruth at an annual Board of Directors meeting.

Center's boys, during which the boys enjoy games of chance, a dunking machine, refreshments, prizes and a raffle. Through its fundraising efforts the association has been financially independent and has been able to support its publication, The Contact, a newsletter that provides current information about alumni and relates information about scheduled events and meetings.

Alumni association members have also helped the Center by speaking at staff training sessions, addressing graduates at the graduation breakfast and ceremony, volunteering at the annual golf tournament and the Vintage Festival in Sonoma, donating a television and VCR to the Hanna school's moral guidance department, and arranging field trips to Air Force bases and naval aircraft carriers. The most valuable contribution of the alumni members, however, has been in serving as positive role models for the boys of Hanna Center.

During the association's early years, Sister Mary Peter served as its moderator—scheduling meetings, publishing minutes, and coordinating activities. After her retirement, Sister Ruth and Bill Byrne assumed responsibilities as moderators. Hanna staff members Dee Jaehrling, Ken Krumdick, Mary Adams and the late John Reilly have been steadfast supporters of the alumni, and Father John Crews makes a point of attending the alumni meetings and special events to lend his support.

In 1999, the alumni association celebrated its 25th anniversary. The association continues to be an invaluable asset to Hanna Center and continues to give hope to the Hanna Center boys.

CHRIS BERGGREN

COURTESY OF DR. KEN LARSEN

Roger Harrison, alumnus

"I'll always be thankful to Hanna Center for what it offered me both in school and in teaching me how to live life in general. I'm thankful to the people I met and to the people who cared about what was happening to the kids around them," said Roger Harrison, while recalling his experience at Hanna.

Born July 12, 1951, in Staten Island, New York, Roger moved with his family to Half Moon Bay, California, when he was two years old. The youngest in a family of three boys and one girl, Roger learned early what it meant to be the son of two alcoholic parents. "My dad was physically abusive to me, my mother and to his mother. I spent more time in foster homes than in my own home because of my parents' drinking problem," recalled Roger.

Lacking supervision, Roger found himself in juvenile hall for various offenses when he was 12 years old. His mother met with Father Regan, who was able to obtain a spot for Roger at Hanna.

Roger remembered the day he arrived: "I fell in love with the place the first time I saw the campus. Hanna was the best thing that happened to me up to that point in my life. I had more opportunities to go places and do things than I would have had in my home life. I got to meet a lot of different boys who had problems similar to mine."

Roger took full advantage of the Hanna program, participating in sports, enjoying field trips and being particularly active in the cottage life. Cottage staff members Ken Krumdick and Jack James influenced him; he felt that Sister Carmel Therese and Sister Virgine took a special interest in his schoolwork. Roger stayed at Hanna for three years, leaving after completing the ninth grade. At graduation Roger received the "The Boy of The Year" award and a Hanna scholarship to attend Serra High School in San Mateo.

After successful completion of high school, Roger joined the U.S. Navy Reserve, earning an honorable discharge. He returned to California and began working in the grocery business. He married his wife Linda in 1970, and they had a son and daughter. Through his affiliation with the Hanna alumni association Roger got help from a fellow alumnus, George Gomes, in obtaining a position in the construction trade in carpentry.

Roger has concentrated on providing his children the family life he did not receive at home. He has been active in coaching sports and in scouting with his son and daughter. Roger believes in giving to his community; as a regular blood donor he has given over 100 pints of blood. A charter member of the Hanna alumni association, Roger was the first member to serve two terms as president. He and

his wife have been mainstays in organizing and conducting the annual carnival for the Hanna boys.

Roger summarizes his experience with Hanna this way: "I've had some difficult times in my life, but I'm happy to say that I've reconciled with my mother and learned to admire her for her strength. I enjoy my wife and my children. I'm happy in my work. All in all, I have a very positive outlook about life, and I'm thankful to Hanna Center for setting me on the right path."

Top left: Roger Harrison at the annual Alumni Carnival.

Above: Roger and Linda Harrison celebrating their 25th wedding anniversary.

The Board of Directors

Hanna Boys Center's 45-member board of directors is responsible for overseeing the operation of the Center. The volunteer board is comprised of people from all walks of life and affords the Center the expertise and information needed to guide its program.

Archbishop John J. Mitty formed the first board in 1946, while the Center was located in Menlo Park, and Eugene Broderick was selected as the first chairman of the board. The board proved to be an invaluable resource in planning the new campus, organizing the fund-raising campaign, and helping with the site evaluation and selection process.

Traditionally, board members have represented an array of professions, including business, agriculture, government, education, community services, construction, and news media. Lawyers, bank vice-presidents, school principals, doctors, dentists, school psychologists, small business owners, financial consultants, and business managers of all kinds have helped shape the Hanna program and provide financial stability to the Center's operation. Every year board members donate countless hours to the Center by sharing their expertise and offering invaluable guidance to the director and Hanna staff.

In addition to the executive committee, which meets monthly, the board is organized into other special committees that concentrate their efforts on particular aspects of the Center's operation. Meeting independently throughout the year are the personnel, finance, education/treatment, audit, legal, long-range planning, membership, public relations and development, and facilities committees. The scholarship committee is a sub-group of the education/treatment committee.

In addition to individual board members' support through memorials and annual gifts, the board as a group has also donated funds for special items for the boys and the Center's facilities as the needs have arisen.

Realizing the value of the individual skills of the board of directors, current executive director Father Crews has sought the aid of their advice and skills frequently. He has devised procedures for investing new members on the board while maintaining the service of the

RUSS FISCHELLA

Top: 1950 Board Chairman Dan Flanagan, left, and Edwin McInnis, 1948–49 chairman.

Above: In 1996 Annette Lomont was the first woman to serve as chairman of the board.

experienced members. He has also promoted the inclusion of women, and was instrumental in selecting the first woman to serve as chair of the board.

Father Crews makes a point of reminding the members each year that the boys are cognizant of the role of the board and that they are very much aware of any board member's presence on campus. Board members tour the grounds, get to know the boys and see them at work at the Center whenever possible.

The annual board meeting each spring is a highlight of the Hanna calendar. Father Crews usually introduces some of the boys currently residing at the Center, or recent graduates, so the board members can hear first-hand accounts of the boys' experiences.

Former chairman of the board James Talton Turner summarized the directors' role this way: "The board has been comprised of generous individuals and business leaders dedicated to providing for the boys and their futures. Whether they review construction of a new cottage, interview boys for scholarships, or provide unique and special incentives for the boys, the time and support they invest in the boys and their programs last a lifetime."

Throughout its history, Hanna Boys Center has been truly blessed by the generous people who have served as members of the board of directors. A complete list of chairmen of the board can be found in Appendix One.

Long-time board member Robert Lynch, publisher of The Sonoma Index-Tribune, with his wife Jean, and Father Crews.

Our Benefactors

Since its inception, Hanna Boys Center has been dependent on generous donors and benefactors. The individual donor has been the mainstay of financial support that has allowed the Center to continue to serve boys and families.

The initial capital campaign to build the campus in Sonoma Valley was characterized by the thorough organization of volunteer fund-raisers in counties and parishes who appealed to parishioners individually. These parishioners responded quickly and generously, meeting and exceeding their campaign goals in a remarkably short timeframe.

This approach—direct appeal to individuals—was formalized by Jim Muldoon, Hanna's first public relations director, who installed a direct mail fund-raising system after the Center opened in Sonoma. This system is still employed today by Hanna's development department, which issues five newsletters each year, plus a Christmas appeal and annual membership renewals. Generous individual donors respond to these appeals with an average donation amount of $19 each. The direct mail appeals and the opportunities for bequests form the nucleus of fund-raising efforts by the development department.

One popular innovation was the establishment of the In Memoriam Fund, which allows family members to honor the memory of loved ones through donations to the Center. The names of the family members are inscribed in an In Memoriam book which is safeguarded in the Center's chapel. One of these books is displayed in the lobby of the administration building, and other books are displayed alternately from time to time. Deceased family members may also be remembered during the celebration of Holy Mass.

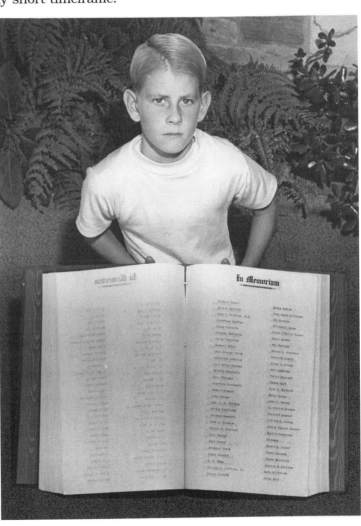

The In Memoriam Book.

During the early years of the Center there were some lean financial times. Monsignor O'Connor spent many hours worrying and praying about finances and how he was going to meet the weekly payroll. Because of increasing construction costs, part of the original scope of the Center's building project had to be postponed. The original plan called for construction of six cottages, but only three were built.

Through the generosity of the building trade union members, three more cottages were built in 1954. The donation of time, labor and materials by these tradesmen and contractors exemplified the sense of mission that has characterized the efforts of Hanna's supporters.

More help was on the way. Generous donations were made to construct other buildings. In 1956, Dr. E. E. Keefe donated a dental clinic. In 1957, Mary Kearney donated the Kearney Auditorium in memory of her husband, Patrick. That same year, the Raskob Foundation donated the Trade School Building. In 1960, the Raskob Foundation donated the infirmary building, named in honor of John J. Raskob. Through the generous donation of Swazi Simmons, tennis courts were constructed and dedicated in 1994.

Board member Swazi Simmons cuts ribbon on new tennis courts.

Throughout the years, numerous celebrities have donated their time, good names and skills in taping public service announcements on behalf of the Center. These announcements have been heard on radio and viewed on television, keeping the mission of Hanna Boys Center in the minds of donors throughout California and other Western states. Bing Crosby, Bob Hope, Arnold Palmer, Jack Lemmon, Paul Anka, Irene Dunne, Gracie Allen, and Barbara Stanwyck are some of the stars who have helped the Center in this manner. (Please see Appendix Six for a complete list of celebrities who have donated public service announcements.)

Members of the medical profession have been equally as generous. Volunteer dentists have donated thousands of hours of service to Hanna's boys, for many of whom the Hanna clinic is their first dental experience. In 1999, 84 volunteer dental professionals participated in meeting the needs of the Center.

Another group of professionals who have been consistent supporters of the Center is the board of directors. In addition to their expertise, board members have given memorials and annual gifts to the Center. Often their gifts are directed to specific needs: one year, it was a van for the new group home; another year, it was furniture for the remodeled cottages. Recently board member Dr. Richard Caselli helped acquire a Panorex X-ray machine from Doctor David Pulsipher. Whatever the particular need of any given year, the board of directors has come through for the Center.

The largest single fund-raising event is the Hanna Boys Center Annual Golf Classic. The golfing tournament began as a "thank you" gesture to the members of the board of directors, and no revenues were generated. But Bob Seymour and Public Relations Director Noel Mertens envisioned greater possibilities and were instrumental in developing this event into a major fund-raiser in 1993. Now in its 7th year, the Golf Classic is renowned as one of the finest benefits conducted in the area and offers an opportunity for Hanna staff, alumni, and board and community members to work together toward a common goal. That the volunteer spirit at Hanna is alive and well is demonstrated yearly in what has become another highlight on the Hanna calendar of events.

Individual volunteers have served Hanna in numerous ways through the years. NBA basketball star Chris Mullen has played ball with the boys, while professional drivers have brought their race cars for

MOULIN STUDIOS

Jimmy Durante with boys.

the boys to view. Football Hall of Fame member Bob St. Clair and comedian Michael Pritchard have spoken to the boys and parents at Hanna open houses. Community members have served as tutors and have helped with administrative duties. Woodcarvers, mechanics, master gardeners, dancers, and performers of all kinds have found time to help the Center and to teach, entertain, instruct and encourage the boys.

Referring to the boys, Father Crews has said, "We are developing winners here."

It's clear that generous people want to help develop winners. Volunteers and donors share the sense of mission and commitment to youth that has been the dream and the reality of Hanna Boys Center since 1946.

Sister Grace greets a boy arriving at Hanna Center.

CHAPTER 6

Timeline
1945–1999

January 21, 1945	Archbishop Hanna Center for Boys pilot program opens in Menlo Park, California.
August 4, 1945	Dedication of Hanna Boys Center, Menlo Park.
March 30, 1946	Articles of Incorporation are signed establishing Hanna Boys Center as a non-profit corporation in the state of California.
October 12, 1946	Boys visit Seals Stadium and meet Lefty O'Doul.
November 12, 1946	Boys watch St. Mary's football team practice and meet star player Herman Wedemeyer.
September 16, 1947	Archbishop Mitty announces purchase of Morris Ranch property in Sonoma.
September 19, 1948	Groundbreaking ceremonies held at the new campus location, Sonoma Valley.
December 4, 1949	First boys move to new campus. There are three cottages: Rosary Hill, Loretto and Mt. Carmel.

1940s

Above: Herman Wedemeyer shows a boy how to pass a football.

Right: Father Regan and Menlo Park boy Jack Piccoli meet San Francisco Seals' manager Lefty O'Doul and catcher Joe Sprinz.

Bottom: Archbishop Mitty dedicates Hanna Boys Center, Menlo Park, August 4, 1945.

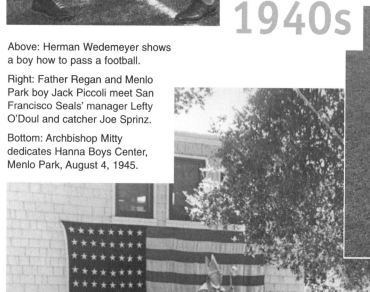

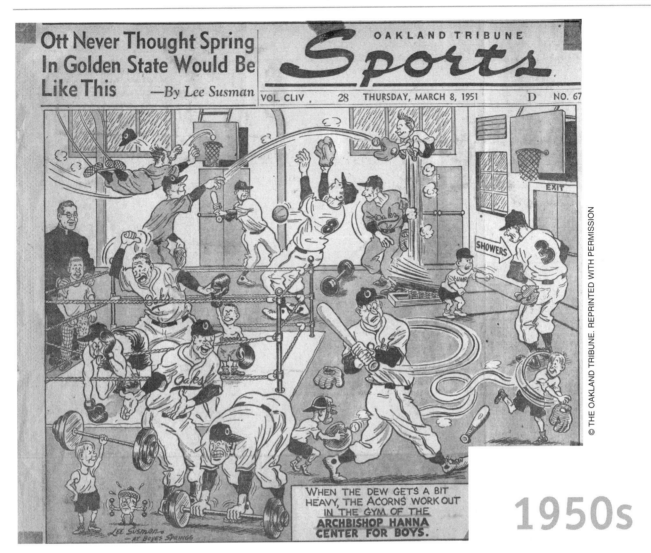

1950s

Top: Cartoon from Oakland Tribune Sports, March 8, 1951.

Above: The first graduating class, June, 1950.

Right: Father Regan with boys and Ralph Edwards on "Truth or Consequences," 1951.

February 26, 1950	The first Mass is offered in Our Lady of Fatima Chapel.
May 21, 1950	The formal dedication of Hanna Boys Center is held.
June 11, 1950	The first class graduates from Hanna Boys Center.
August 12, 1950	The first field day competition is held.
December 8, 1950	The stations of the cross (sculpted by Ruth Cravath) are installed in the chapel.
February 1, 1951	Hanna boys appear on the TV show "Truth or Consequences," hosted by Ralph Edwards.
February 5, 1951	Basketball great Hank Luisetti conducts a clinic at the Center.
March, 1951	The Oakland Oaks baseball team trains at the Center.
March 9, 1951	49er quarterback Frankie Albert visits the Center.
March 18, 1951	Hanna boys meet Hopalong Cassidy at the San Francisco Cow Palace.
June 19, 1951	The crucifix corpus (sculpted by Ruth Cravath) is installed in the chapel.
August 10, 1951	Hanna boys meet Heavyweight Champion Joe Louis.
August 13, 1951	President Harry S. Truman sends a letter to Father O'Connor.

1950s

LARRY KENNEY

THE WHITE HOUSE

WASHINGTON

August 13, 1951

Dear Father O'Connor:

I regret exceedingly that I cannot accept your cordial invitation to visit Hanna Center for Boys when I go to San Francisco in connection with the signing of the peace treaty with Japan. Already I have had to decline several other invitations because of the very limited time I shall be absent from Washington.

I can think of nothing more worthy of Archbishop Hanna that this living memorial bearing his honored name. May I, in thanking you for the invitation, express the hope that this work in behalf of future citizens may long grow and prosper.

Very sincerely yours

Harry S. Truman

Reverend William L. O'Connor
Director
Hanna Center for Boys
P.O. Box 100
Sonoma, California

Clockwise from photo above: Frankie Albert at Hanna.

Joe DiMaggio visits Hanna.

Harry Zohn and Freddie Starr meet Hopalong Cassidy (William Boyd).

Letter from President Harry S. Truman.

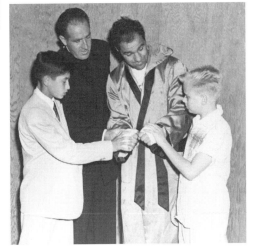

January 2, 1952	Boxer Eddie Chavez visits the Center.
April 2, 1953	Sacred Heart sculpture (by Ruth Cravath) is installed in the chapel.
December 21, 1953	Madonna and Child statue (by Ruth Cravath) is installed in the chapel.
January 23, 1954	Middleweight Champion Bobo Olson fights Joe Rindone at Winterland, San Francisco, in a benefit bout for the Center.
June 20, 1954	Three new cottages are dedicated: Notre Dame, St. Joseph's, and Mt. Alverno.
February, 1955	Hanna boys meet Abbott and Costello.
May, 1955	Hanna boys and Father Regan meet Rocky Marciano.

Clockwise from top left: Boxer Eddie Chavez visits with the boys before one of his benefit bouts for the Center.

Movie star Pat O'Brien ("Knute Rockne") shows the boys how to bunt.

Abbott and Costello "doggin' it" with Father Regan and boys.

Heavyweight champion Rocky Marciano shows his fists to Father Regan and boys.

Former heavyweight champion Max Baer and Father Regan.

Paul Brown, head coach, Cleveland Browns.

September 1, 1955	The trade school building opens.
September 15, 1955	The school addition of three classrooms opens.
June 21, 1956	President Dwight D. Eisenhower sends a letter to Father O'Connor thanking him for a trout rod and flies.
October 2, 1956	The 500th boy enrolls at Hanna.
May 19, 1957	Dedication of the Kearney Auditorium and Raskob Trade School is held.
June 2, 1957	Monsignor O'Connor celebrates the silver jubilee of his priesthood.

Clockwise from top: Father O'Connor greets 500th boy to enroll at Hanna.

Eighth anniversary of the Center, December 4, 1957.

Willie Mays with Father Cox and John Hines at Seals Stadium.

Letter from President Dwight D. Eisenhower.

THE WHITE HOUSE

WASHINGTON

June 21, 1956

Dear Father O'Connor:

I am grateful to you, to Jerry McCray, and to all the residents of the Hanna Boys Center, for your kind thoughtfulness in sending me a fishing rod that I know I shall enjoy using, a nice assortment of trout flies, and a silver card of life membership in the Sonoma Golf and Country Club. All these things are calculated to take me for a little while out of my hospital room and remind me of some of the pleasures I hope to have later in the summer.

Thank you, too, for sending me the brochure on the Center; I have read with interest of the work you are doing.

Sincerely,

Dwight D. Eisenhower

P.S. Mrs. Eisenhower appreciates very much the earrings that you enclosed for her.

Right Reverend William L. O'Connor
Director, Hanna Boys Center
Post Office Box 100
Sonoma, California

ORIE DAMEWOOD

February, 1958   Hanna boys meet comedian Joe E. Brown.

April 8, 1958   Father Gerald Cox is appointed assistant director. Father Thomas Regan is appointed director of Catholic Social Services, San Mateo.

June 27, 1958   Hanna boys meet San Francisco Giants and Willie Mays at Seals Stadium.

Clockwise from above: Comedian Joe E. Brown bowls one for the boys.

George "Papa Bear" Halas, coach and owner of the Chicago Bears, attended Mass at Hanna chapel with members of his team during a time out from their training camp in Sonoma.

The boys are all ears for Willie.

Ninth anniversary of Hanna Boys Center.

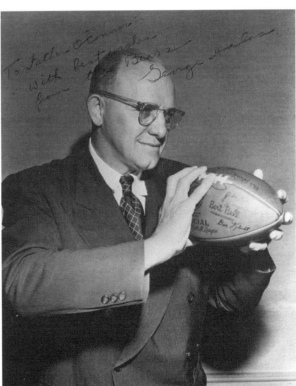

May 10, 1960	The infirmary building is dedicated.
April 8, 1961	Hanna boys meet comedian George Gobel.
February 21, 1962	Hanna Boys Center becomes part of the newly created Diocese of Santa Rosa.
March 4, 1962	Father John J. O'Hare is appointed assistant director.
May 20, 1962	Major League umpire Ralph "Babe" Pinelli visits the Center.
May 24, 1962	The stained glass window is installed in the chapel.
July 13, 1964	Father James Barry, former director of Hanna Center, Menlo Park, dies.
November, 1964	Hanna boys meet Tennessee Ernie Ford.
January 28, 1965	The 1,000th boy enrolls at Hanna.
February 11, 1967	Hanna boys meet Hall of Fame baseball player Frank Robinson.

ORIE DAMEWOOD

Clockwise from top: George Gobel salutes Hanna boy.

Football Hall-of-Famer Y. A. Tittle visits the Center.

Ralph "Babe" Pinelli, "Mr. Ump," shows David Narvaez and board chairman Dan Flanagan the face mask he used in calling Don Larsen's perfect game in the 1956 World Series.

Notre Dame football coach Ara Parsegian takes time out to talk with associate director Father John O'Hare.

February 17, 1965	Bing Crosby records a public service announcement for Hanna.
February 27, 1967	Father O'Connor meets President Nixon at Marco Island, Florida, at the Tony Lema Memorial Golf Tournament.
June 18, 1967	The statue "The Boy" is dedicated.
March 28, 1968	The Napa group home opens.
October 1, 1968	Father Gregory A. Klaas is appointed assistant director.
December 3, 1969	Boys move into the Santa Rosa group home.

Clockwise from top: The Smothers Brothers.

Hall-of-Famer Frank Robinson talks with boys (from left) David Dominguez, Tom Marquez, Tim Bennick and Richard Owens at the Townehouse Hotel, San Francisco. Frank was honored that night as the Associated Press Male Athlete of the Year, February 11, 1967.

Frank Mackle, President Richard Nixon, golf pro Gene Sarazen and Monsignor O'Connor chat at the Tony Lema Memorial Tournament, Marco Island, Florida, February 27, 1967.

1960s

VANO-WELLS-FAGLIANO PHOTOGRAPHY

June 22, 1970	Father James E. Pulskamp is appointed assistant director.
September 9, 1970	Governor Ronald Reagan visits the Center.
September 6, 1971	Boys move into the Petaluma group home.
October 1, 1972	Monsignor O'Connor steps down as director. He is succeeded by Father James Pulskamp.
June 26, 1973	The 1,500th boy enrolls at Hanna.
January 2, 1974	Snow falls at Hanna Center.
May 18, 1974	The Hanna Boys Center Alumni Association holds its first meeting.
June, 1975	President Gerald Ford sends a letter to Hanna graduates.
April 30, 1977	The ranch program is officially phased out.

PATRICK PERROTT

1970s

ORIE DAMEWOOD

PATRICK PERROTT

Above: Snow at Hanna?

Right: Letter from President Gerald Ford.

Opposite page, clockwise from top:

Then-Governor of California Ronald Reagan visits the boys at Hanna Center.

49er Abe Woodson tells the boys about life in the NFL.

Hanna Center rancher George Winkler gives advice to a lad on the ranch.

THE WHITE HOUSE

WASHINGTON

TO THE 1975 HIGH SCHOOL GRADUATES:

As high school graduates, you are passing an important milestone. You are about to enter into a society that is filled with challenge and opportunity. What you do with your lives from this point forward will determine not only your personal self-fulfillment, but the general well-being of our nation.

You carry with you the hopes of those who know and trust you. The future of America depends on your generation. You can make of America whatever you want. The opportunities before you are as great as the challenges.

Education is the greatest key to a better life. But to open the door of opportunity you need faith in yourselves, pride in what you have accomplished, and the idealism to persevere. If you add to this the awareness that learning never ceases, you will indeed bring to your lives the kind of meaning and satisfaction you seek.

I wish you every success on the road ahead.

Gerald R. Ford

1980s

Clockwise from top: Hall-of-Famer Willie McCovey records a public service announcement (PSA) for the Center.

Actress Lynn Redgrave also donated a PSA for the Center.

Bob Hope, another PSA donor and Hanna supporter.

October 19, 1980	The first alumni sponsored field day is held, dedicated to Jim Healy.
February 12, 1982	The Santa Rosa group home closes, ending the off-campus group home program.
June 6, 1982	Monsignor O'Connor celebrates his golden jubilee as a priest.
December 15, 1983	Father John S. Crews is named associate director.
July 1, 1984	Father John Crews is appointed director. Monsignor O'Connor retires. Father Pulskamp is named chancellor of the diocese.
February, 1985	Hanna Boys Center purchases property at 710 Agua Caliente Road.
July 7, 1986	Boys move into the new on-campus group home (Father O'Connor House).
1987	Television personalities Steve Allen, Robert Blake, and Dana Carvey record public service announcements for Hanna.
August 13, 1987	Willie McCovey donates a public service announcement.
July 6, 1988	The 2,000th boy enrolls at Hanna.
1989	San Francisco 49ers Randy Cross and Delvin Williams donate public service announcements for Hanna.
October 31, 1989	Bob Hope donates a public service announcement.
December 3, 1989	Mass of Thanksgiving is offered and Hanna's 40th anniversary is celebrated.

Top: Invitation to the 40th Anniversary Mass of Thanksgiving.

Bottom: "Two old friends"—our co-founders, 1982.

The Board of Directors
and
Father John S. Crews
Executive Director
of

Hanna Boys Center

cordially invite you to attend

**The 40th Anniversary
Mass of Thanksgiving**

celebrated by
The Most Reverend John T. Steinbock, D.D.
Bishop of Santa Rosa, California

**Sunday, December 3, 1989
10:00 A.M.**

Our Lady of Fatima Chapel
HANNA BOYS CENTER
17000 Arnold Drive
Sonoma, California 95476

March 29, 1990	President George W. Bush sends Hanna Center a photograph of himself jogging in a Hanna sweatshirt.
May 14, 1990	Paul Anka donates a public service announcement.
July 5, 1990	The Sisters of St. Francis depart Hanna Boys Center for the motherhouse in Milwaukee, Wisconsin.
September 6, 1990	George Seifert donates a public service announcement.
November 20, 1990	Leslie Nielsen donates a public service announcement.
March 20, 1991	The Western Association of Schools and Colleges grants accreditation to the Hanna school.
August 28, 1991	Boys move into the St. Francis Cottage.
December 30, 1991	Monsignor William O'Connor dies.
April 6, 1993	Johnny Miller donates a public service announcement.
November 16, 1993	San Francisco 49er quarterback Steve Young records a public service announcement for the Center and meets with three Hanna boys.

1990s

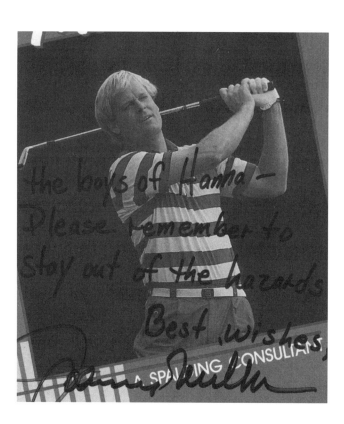

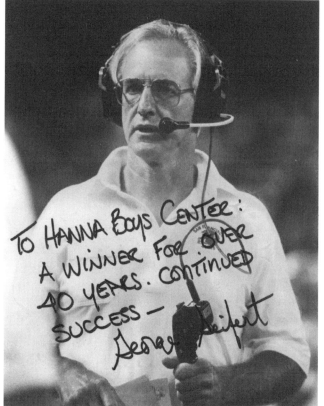

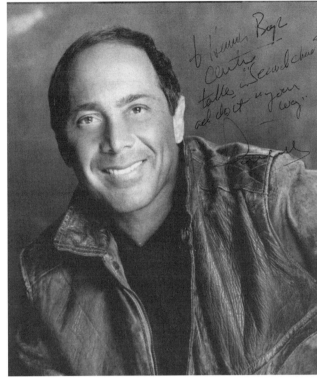

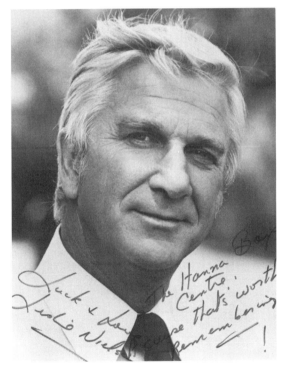

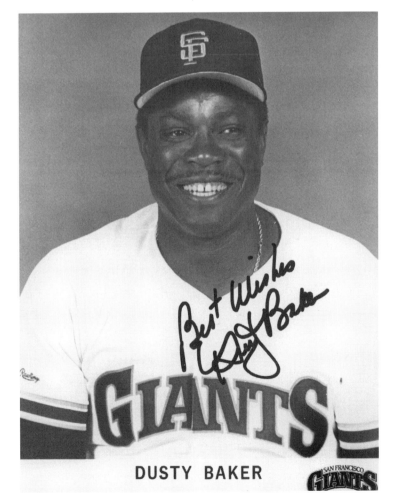

DUSTY BAKER

Opposite page from top: President George Bush jogging in his Hanna Center shirt.

49er coach George Seifert donated a PSA for the Center.

Golfing great Johnny Miller.

This page, clockwise from top left: 49er quarterback Steve Young took time out to meet with our boys and to record a PSA.

Paul Anka helped out also.

SF Giants Manager Dusty Baker contributed a PSA.

Leslie Nielsen got his PSA done on the first take.

February 24, 1994	The tennis courts are dedicated.
December 4, 1994	The second on-campus group home (Father Flanagan House) is dedicated by Monsignor William Flanagan.
December 29, 1994	Monsignor William Flanagan dies.
June 24, 1996	The 2,500th boy enrolls at Hanna.
March 7, 1997	The Western Association of Schools and Colleges grants a six year accreditation to the Hanna school.
April 28, 1998	The City Council of Rohnert Park presents Hanna with a resolution of support and honor.
June 22, 1999	The 2,700th boy enrolls at Hanna.
December 4, 1999	The 50th Anniversary of Hanna Boys Center.

Clockwise from top: Pat Paulsen took time out from his "presidential campaign" to record a PSA for the Center.

Comedian Michael Pritchard has spoken at Hanna open houses.

Arnold Palmer wearing a Hanna Hawks hat in tournament play. Arnold was kind enough to record PSAs on two occasions for the Center.

Appendix 1

Chairmen of the Board of Directors

1946	Eugene Broderick	1964	L. George Lambert	1982	William McInerney, Esq.
1947	Eugene Broderick	1965	Oliver V. Merle	1983	Fred R. Grant
1948	Edwin McInnis	1966	Homer Helmstein	1984	Fred R. Grant
1949	Edwin McInnis	1967	John Lounibos	1985	John E. Schaeffer
1950	Daniel V. Flanagan	1968	Roger M. Murray	1986	Joseph P. Donnelly
1951	Daniel V. Flanagan	1969	Robert E. Maloney	1987	James E. Jensen
1952	Joseph A. Murphy	1970	Emile Maloney	1988	Robert D. Rossi
1953	Charles L. Harney	1971	Thomas F. Poggi	1989	Louis J. Geissberger, D.D.S.
1954	Charles L. Harney	1972	Melvin Lewis	1990	Paul M. Watson
1955	Charles L. Harney	1973	Melvin G. Lewis	1991	William E. McDonnell
1956	Frank J. Perry	1974	Marvin E. Cardoza	1992	Robert J. Kenneth
1957	Frank J. Perry	1975	Arthur C. Latno, Jr.	1993	Peter D. Ashe, Esq.
1958	Sidney A. Haag	1976	James A. Scatena	1994	Harry B. Arbios
1959	Sidney A. Haag	1977	Albert A. Maggini	1995	James Talton Turner, III
1960	Thomas Lucas	1978	Robert F. Lautze	1996	Annette E. Lomont
1961	J. Warnock Walsh	1979	Alfred G. Cinelli	1997	L. Wayne Batmale
1962	Arthur J. Melka	1980	Vincent J. Sullivan	1998	William H. McInerney, Jr., Esq.
1963	George Doherty	1981	Elwood B. Lang	1999	Richard L. Robinson

Appendix 2

Sisters of St. Francis—Years of Service at Hanna Boys Center

Mother Mary Bartholomew, 1955–60
Sister Alberta, 1960–63
Sister Allan Marie, 1955–68
Sister Aloysine, 1968–84
Sister Ann Dorothy, 1964–65
Sister Ann Lawrence, 1975–83
Sister Anna Marie, 1961–66
Sister Augusta, 1955–60
Sister Carlene, 1950–51
Sister Carmel Therese, 1957–64
Sister Charity, 1949
Sister Cordelia, 1960–81
Sister Edwardine, 1967–87
Sister Elizabeth, 1952–67
Sister Ellen, 1955–59
Sister Francis Xavier, 1965–66

Sister Hildegarde, 1975–82
Sister Jean Clare, 1966–67
Sister Joan, 1982–88
Sister Joanna, 1954
Sister Johnita, 1954
Sister Madeleva, 1949
Sister Marie de Lourdes, 1966–67
Sister Mary Alfred, 1964
Sister Mary Clare, 1949–79
Sister Mary Claude, 1985
Sister Mary Ferdinanda, 1949
Sister Mary Grace, 1949–66; 1970–84
Sister Mary Immaculate, 1973–74;
    1978–79; 1984–88
Sister Mary Lawrence, 1977
Sister Mary Louis, 1965

Sister Mary Peter, 1950–59; 1970–88
Sister Marysia, 1951–53
Sister Michaella, 1952–54; 1975–76
Sister Mona, 1951–63
Sister Olive, 1967
Sister Patricia, 1968
Sister Peter Claver, 1950–55
Sister Philomene, 1960–64
Sister Regina, 1949–52
Sister Renee, 1968
Sister Romuald, 1971–73
Sister Ruth, 1983–Present
Sister Thomas Mary, 1967
Sister Vianney, 1953
Sister Virgine, 1961–67
Sister Yvonne Therese, 1955–63

Appendix 3

Donors of Public Service Announcements

Hanna Boys Center is grateful to the following celebrities for donating their talents in taping public service announcements.

Claude Akins
Gracie Allen
Steve Allen
Paul Anka
Dusty Baker
Robert Blake
Ann Blythe
George Burns
Dana Carvey
Jackie Cooper
Bob Crane
Bing Crosby

Randy Cross
Bob Cummings
Dennis Day
Joe DiMaggio
Irene Dunne
Ralph Edwards
Tennessee Ernie Ford
Dan Gladden
George Gobel
Charleton Heston
Bob Hope
Jack Lemmon
Huey Lewis
Art Linkletter
Bob Lurie
Groucho Marx

Willie McCovey
Johnny Miller
Chris Mullen
Ozzie and Harriet Nelson
Leslie Nielsen
Arnold Palmer
Pat Paulsen
Lynn Redgrave
George Siefert
Tommy Smothers
Barbara Stanwyck
Danny Thomas
Ken Venturi
Delvin Williams
Steve Young

Appendix 4

Outstanding Boy of the Year

1978	Steven C. Ullrich
1979	Darren Vorrath
1980	Darren Vorrath
1981	Rob Khan
1982	Sean Stevens
1983	Steven Markel
1984	Les Melghem
1985	Jeff Kirk
1986	William Conley
1987	Khai Banh
1988	Brad Howard
1989	William Gunnells
1990	Jeff Pardi
1991	Vilavong Tongvanh
1992	Sout Phavasiri
1993	Michael Kinsley
1994	Adam Mancebo
1995	John Butler
1996	Somkhit Thongban
1997	Vanna Chaiyasith
1998	Jeremy Cates
1999	Chris Asaro

Vanna Chaiyasith, Boy of the Year, 1997.

Chris Asaro receives the Boy of the Year Award from Father Crews, 1999.

Appendix 5

Donors to the Haven of Hope Fund

Employees
Mary C. Adams
Mario F. Alioto III
Anonymous
Jerry Borchelt
Ronald C. Bridgeman
Steve Cederborg
Monica S. Clark
Gloria Coleman
Mr. and Mrs. Joseph Filice
Kathy Gray
Keith Hale
Jim and Becky Hiss
Linda C. Klein
Duane Kobza and Darla Brocco Kobza
The Lourdeaux Family
Barbara Jean Merle
Eileen M. Meuris, Ed.D.
Robert Miller
Timothy J. Norman, Ph.D.
George and Kathryn Perry
Paula A. O'Callaghan
Joan Rossetti
Diane Ruggles (Woodcock)
C. Richard Russell
D. Scott and Donna Singer
Sisters of St. Francis of Assisi
Donavon Skalicky
Norm and Marge Stewart
Patricia Taylor

Special thanks to Mrs. James Healy for her generous support.

Friends of Hanna
Mrs. Donald F. Canevari
Michael V. Merle
Paul Van Ek
In Memory of Joseph Nozzolillo

Board of Directors
Sophie Lei Aldrich
Harry B. Arbios
Dan Benedetti
Thomas E. Bertelsen, Jr.
Jack R. Bertges
Sister Linda Ann Cahill, D.C.
Richard O. Caselli, D.D.S.
Charles Corsiglia
Randall B. DeVoto
Terence A. DeVoto
Donald M. Feehan
Jack Fitzpatrick
John E. Fox
Arthur Fritz, Jr.
Bob Greenbaum
Louis Geissberger
James Hengehold
Peter Imperial
Robert Kenneth
Daniel Libarle
Thomas J. Lohwasser, Ed.D.

Annette E. Lomont
Dexter Louie, M.D.
Robert M. Lynch
Albert A. Maggini
Jane McClure
William E. McDonnell
William H. McInerney, Jr., Esq.
Cathy Murphy
Pete and Joanne Murphy
Eugene Payne, III, Esq.
Vincent L. Pelfini
Thomas M. Perkins
Michael Pescatello
Thomas Peterson
Mary Jo Potter
Richard L. Robinson
Caroline "Swazi" Simmons
Robert E. Simms, Esq.
Vincent J. Sullivan
David A. Thompson
Eugene Traverso
James Talton Turner III
Paul Watson

Appendix 6

Staff with Long Service

Carl Ringo, financial officer 1972–94
21 years of service.

Ron Bridgeman, teacher
1969–present; 30 years of service.

Donavon Skalicky, teacher
1968–present; 31 years of service.

Mary Adams, secretary
1967–present; 33 years of service.

Bob Vitt, CCW, rec staff, transportation
1963–present; 37 years of service.

Patrick Perrott, CCW, rec staff, manager
of residences, information services
1969–present; 30 years of service.

Amy Heggie, bookkeeper, 1959–86;
27 years of service.

Jerry Borchelt, CCW, teacher
1970–present; 29 years of service.

Lee Schmidt, maintenance
1975–present; 25 years of service.

Not pictured: Dorothy Boche, clerical
staff 1951–77; 26 years of service.

Appendix 7

Presidents of the Alumni Association

1974–76	John Brown	1988–90	Norbert Anzano
1976–78	Myron MacNeil	1990–92	Al Haggett
1978–80	Al Carli	1992–94	Al Haggett
1980–82	George Gomes	1994–96	James Markel
1982–84	Roger Harrison	1996–98	James Markel
1984–86	Roger Harrison	1998–2000	Ken Murphy
1986–88	John Brown		

Norbert Anzano and wife Jane.

James Markel and wife Irene.

Myron MacNeil and Sister Peter.

Ken Murphy with Rene and Andrew.

NED DAVIS

Acknowledgements

There were many contributors to this book—some voluntary and some involuntary.

My special thanks are given to Bob Lynch, publisher of The Sonoma Index-Tribune and long-time Hanna board member, who helped develop the book outline, conducted several interviews, wrote three profiles, proofread the manuscript and created the book's title. He also told me, "Yes, you need a firm schedule, and stick to it." Bob gave me the encouragement and confidence I needed to complete the project.

Many thanks to Dolores Jaehrling, who wrote the profiles on the sisters and developed the history of the Sisters of St. Francis at Hanna, contributing a valuable perspective that otherwise could not have been included. She also read the manuscript for historical accuracy.

I will miss pestering Ann Healy and seeing her eyes light up each time I asked her a question about Hanna's history. This "lovable, living library" has kept meticulous notes about Hanna milestones and has preserved historical photos and information that otherwise would have been lost.

I am grateful that the book editor, Catherine Thorpe, was gentle with her changes and suggestions, was solid with her recommendations, and wrote more than most editors normally would during the early part of the project.

I never doubted Nan Perrott's ability to design the book and to lay it out beautifully. Nan also contributed her editing and proofreading skills. Gina Bostian made the jacket design fun, and the results exciting. Thanks to both.

Chris Berggren of Custom Images was very generous in scanning more than 280 photographs for this project, and his wife Jules' reactions to the photos were often the litmus test for inclusion in the book.

Diane Smith of the Sonoma Valley Historical Society helped find photographs of early Sonoma Valley. Jeffrey Burns of the San Francisco Archdiocese Archives was most responsive in obtaining a photo of the Menlo Park dedication.

Many thanks to Hanna staff members Jim Thompson, Debbie Drummond, Jim McLees and Sister Ruth, who contributed photos in cartons, albums, binders, cigar boxes, envelopes, and shoeboxes. Thanks to Barbara Merle and Lori Hines, who helped collect needed information. Steve Cederborg garnered the funds to produce the book, and he also read the manuscript.

Many thanks to all former and current Hanna staff members who wrote newsletters, press releases, yearbooks, brochures, pamphlets, annual reports, studies, "Hanna Haps" and correspondence of any kind—I stole their work with impunity and without much embarrassment.

Thank you, Father Crews, for assigning the job to me and granting me the time to do it.

Finally, I am grateful to my ebullient wife, Angelina, who was encouraging to me throughout the project and never once said, "I'm tired of hearing about that book."

—Bill Byrne

Notes on Sources

Interviews

Hanna Personnel
Father John S. Crews
Sister Ruth Gardner
Mrs. Ann Healy
Mr. Ken Krumdick
Ms. Dolores Jaehrling
Sister Mary Peter
Monsignor James E. Pulskamp

Hanna Alumni
Norbert Anzano
John Benedetti
John Brown
Al Carli
Tom Chin
Bill Conley
Harry Dillon
Ray Doherty
George Gomes

Al Haggett
Roger Harrison
Myron MacNeil
Noma Martini
Frank Youngblood

Other Interview
Mrs. James Muldoon

Newspapers and Periodicals
Hanna Haps, 1948–1975
San Francisco Chronicle, 1946–1952
San Francisco Examiner, 1946–1959
The Monitor, 1945–1947
The Oakland Tribune, 1951–1952
The Press Democrat, 1949–1999
The Redwood Crozier, 1983
Referee Magazine, 1952
The Sonoma Index-Tribune, 1946–1999

Books
Hanousek, Sister Mary Eunice, O.S.F., *A New Assisi*, The Bruce Publishing Company, Milwaukee, WI, 1948.

McNamara, Robert F., "Archbishop Hanna, Rochesterian," *Rochester History*, Rochester Public Library, April, 1963.